Never Cheat a Holy Man

A memoir

by Joyce Mueller

Copyright © 2012 Joyce Mueller

All rights reserved.

ISBN: 1532845685
ISBN-13: 978-1532845680

DEDICATION

For my three sons, the hearts of my heart

CONTENTS

ACKNOWLEDGMENTS vii
CHAPTER 1 **THE LURE OF SWEET SPICES** 1
CHAPTER 2 **FANTASY SHAKE UP** 5
CHAPTER 3 **ASIAN REALITY**..9
CHAPTER 4 **A PROFUSION OF MALES**...................................14
CHAPTER 5 **TUNING IN** 20
CHAPTER 6 **RUBBISH GIVERS; RUBBISH REMOVERS**.........27
CHAPTER 7 **ONE COOL CHICKEN** 30
CHAPTER 8 **COLD TOAST AND HOT TEA** 34
CHAPTER 9 **EAST PAKISTAN HINDU FAIR** 40
CHAPTER 10 **NEVER CHEAT A HOLY MAN** 45
CHAPTER 11 **MODHU, RIKI TIKI TAVI of BENGAL** 47
CHAPTER 12 **THE GO-DOWN INCIDENT** 50
CHAPTER 13 **MODHU, DECORATOR** 54
CHAPTER 14 **TO MARKET, TO MARKET** 57
CHAPTER 15 **NO EXCUSES SHORT OF PLAGUE OR RABIES**63
CHAPTER 16 **MODHU TO THE RESCUE** 68
CHAPTER 17 **THE SNAKE AND THE DRAGON LADY** 71
CHAPTER 18 **ARE YOU SLEEPING, SISTER MARIE, SISTER MARIE?**..76
CHAPTER 19 **OL' NO NOSE**...82
CHAPTER 20 **"TUNDA" IN THE MOUNTAINS** 85
CHAPTER 21 **"THIS MEANS WAR"** 91
CHAPTER 22 **CASE CLOSED** 98
CHAPTER 23 **TIME TO FLY** 102

CHAPTER 24	**PARANOIA**	108
CHAPTER 25	**INTRIGUE IN BENGAL**	111
CHAPTER 26	**WEL-CUM MEMSAB**	119
CHAPTER 27	**SHOCK CONTROL**	128
CHAPTER 28	**DARING DELECTABLES**	132
CHAPTER 29	**DR. CHAND'S SURPRISE**	135
CHAPTER 30	**ONE VERY HOT NIGHT**	140
CHAPTER 31	**THE RED CARPET**	143
EPILOGUE — FAREWELL TO BENGAL		151

ACKNOWLEDGMENTS

The stories in this memoir are based on true events, as I saw and felt them during the three years I lived in Southeast Asia with my teen-aged sons and my husband. A special acknowledgment goes to "Doc," who took us with him on an adventure far beyond our accustomed American safety net.

We learned to balance the tragedies of poverty and disease that confronted us daily with the humor of everyday situations that confounded us. We discovered that people are the same, with the same needs and loves, no matter their culture.

If I could throw a great waft of "thank you's" into the sky, they would still not reach all of the dear folk who have lent their personal stories, their insightful critiques, and their constant support. I must name just a few: Donna, without whose encouragement in the beginning I would not have been brave enough to forge ahead; May and Weld and Elma, who listened with endless patience to every editing, every re-write; Rosaria, Anne, Abbie, Andrea, Bill, Peggy, Russ, Ginney, John, Lily, Martha, Mary, Mike and Terry of the Bandon Writers Group—so supportive, such great listeners and thoughtful critiquers; Karen, who was generous and helpful with her editing. Most of all, abundant thanks go to my own dear family of brother and sisters, sons, and grandchildren, who have heard many of the stories in one form or another —and have encouraged, cajoled, corrected—and clapped. Bless 'em.

And a special thanks to Weld Champneys for the "Holy Man" cover image, to Ginney Etherton and Donn Davy for book editing and printing.

I love remembering, and hope my readers will laugh and cry at the stories, as I still do.

Joyce Mueller
Port Orford, Oregon
June 1, 2016

Joyce Mueller

PART ONE

You cannot cross the sea
merely by staring at the water.
                                                           -Rabindranath Tagore

CHAPTER 1 **THE LURE OF SWEET SPICES**

"I'll have pheasant under glass, please," I said, with the reckless abandon of one who is not paying the bill.

"Ignore prices," our host had graciously told my husband and me. "Order whatever you want."

It was hard to ignore any of the prices in this elegant restaurant of Sausalito. My choice, not at all the most expensive item on the menu, could almost pay for a girder of the nearby Golden Gate Bridge.

The superbly prepared food, the selection of fine wines, the host's suave manners and smooth voice—all stage-setting for "the pitch." The pitcher was Dr. Rehass from the University of Chicago. It was his job to lure my professor husband into accepting a two-year appointment in East Pakistan. That country was requesting an advisor for their teacher-training program, my husband's area of expertise. Ford Foundation was the financial backer, with University of Chicago supervising.

Many worries popped into my mind as the man talked. 'We've just moved into our new house. Settling in has been hard enough, but with my nursing job, plus the responsibility of caring for our three teen-aged sons, it would be a tough go without Doc's help. He teaches the boys "guy stuff," such as car and house repair, and they can talk sports for hours. I don't know those things. It's important for them to have him nearby at this time in their lives. Still, if this position is something he truly wants, feels challenged by, how can I stand in his way?' I tried to smother any other feelings.

"And, Joyce," Dr. Rehass broke into my troubled thoughts, "Ford Foundation prefers that the family of the new advisor goes with him. You will all be made as comfortable as possible, and of course, schooling will be arranged for your sons."

I held my breath, hardly daring to believe that he was offering me a ticket to the land of my most precious fantasies. When I was a young girl, I often roamed the prairies of my North Dakota home, dreaming the billowy clouds into magic carpets that carried me off to exotic India. I swayed to the rhythms of twanging sitars and husky pan-pipes. A darkly handsome maharajah in flowing silk robes wooed me with passion fruits and sweet wine. Silent servants padded in and out of the palace salon, bowing before us as they did the master's bidding.

Dr. Rehass kept breaking into my dream sequence with reality details. It was most annoying. He was describing East Pakistan as being heavily populated, desperately poor.

"The flat delta lands with their many rivers flood every year during monsoon storms and tropical gales. Many thousands starve to death or die of diseases such as cholera, typhoid fever or tuberculosis."

This was my exotic India he was talking about. I knew just a little about India's history, enough to know that this East Pakistan place, although still East Bengal, was no longer a part of India. In 1947, the British Commonwealth gave India its independence. Many of the Muslims who lived in West Bengal moved to East Bengal. Hindus in East Bengal moved to West Bengal. Muslims and Hindus of other parts of India also changed places, amid terrible strife, but the Muslims now had their own nation, named Pakistan. To me, it was still my exotic India, but with a new name. I didn't like to hear all those bad, sad things Dr. Rehass was saying.

"Joyce," the smooth voice again, "you will be a *memsahib* and your husband will be a *sahib*. Your sons will be *chota* (small) *sahibs*."

That sounded more like it! I had read about the sahibs of Kipling's India. *Sahib* was used as a title of respect, most often for white people, similar to "sir." A *memsahib* was his wife.

As we parted that evening, Dr. Rehass said, "I hope to hear soon that you will be joining the Ford Foundation advisors and their families."

No doubt in my mind, I wanted to be a memsahib. And my teacher husband sounded eager to meet the challenge of the new teaching assignment. It might be a tougher decision for our sons, who had just begun to make new friends in their new schools in a new town. They loved having their own rooms in their brand new home. They had gone without many things that their peers took for granted. They had helped to keep the family going by taking on jobs, even at their young ages, so that their father could further his education. We would need to talk this over as a family. Our sons should have a major part in the decision making.

"Yeah! I don't have to start university right away." This from our oldest son, Donn, who was just graduating from high school, and was eager to test the world.

When Douglas, seventeen months younger, heard that there was no high school for him in Dacca, where we would be living, he said, "That's OK. My choice would be to go to the American International School in New Delhi, India. I know other kids from Davis who go there, and our friend, Dr. Newland will be the new principal. It won't be too strange, I guess."

I was delighted that Doug had chosen this excellent school on his own. He would be among friends right from the start. But it suddenly hit me that India really was a different country than Pakistan, and my son would be there, not with me. My fantasy was fading.

Steven, age 12, had been reading Kipling's Jungle Book. Animal lover that he was, he had become entranced by the character of Riki Tiki Tavi, a mongoose. "If I can have a pet mongoose, I'll go any place you want! Oh, boy, a mongoose!" And he raced away to tell his friends.

So it was settled. We gave notice to our employers; sold our new home; sold our new car; sold, stored, or packed our belongings in preparation for new educational experiences and grand adventures.

We were an electrically charged family of five, jabbering our fantasies, as we boarded the huge Pan American airplane at San Francisco International Airport in the summer of 1964. We flew from Hawaii to Japan to Hong Kong, Taiwan, Thailand, and New Delhi, where we left our dear Douglas (and a broken-off piece of my heart) at his new boarding school. Then on to Karachi, West Pakistan, and finally Dacca, East Pakistan. It was to be our home away from home for the next three, not two years, as in the original contract. And three years beyond that, in West Pakistan. But that's another story.

CHAPTER 2 **FANTASY SHAKE UP**

"Passengers! You will buckle into your seats NOW." The pilot's deep voice came over the loud speaker with force. "Pakistan International Airlines will arrive Dacca in ten minutes, InshaAllah," [God willing].

The petite Pakistan Airlines hostess, her face tight with distress, tried to settle the passengers.

"Please to sit! Please to sit!" she pleaded in her high, timid voice.

Most of the passengers ignored her, continuing to tug at their overhead luggage while pushing against one another with their hips or shoulders. The most successful shovers juggled into the best positions for the exit line-up.

The pilot's voice erupted from the loud speaker. "People, we cannot land until all passengers are seated!"

The plane began to circle, dipping at a sharp enough angle to force the standing passengers back into their seats. The rest of us could finally see down below.

"Look, Mom!" My young son pointed toward the ground. "There isn't anything but water with a few shredded-wheat-looking huts sitting on top. Where will we land?"

"Doesn't look very promising, does it? But the pilot just said we were about to land so something solid must be down there." I hoped I sounded more certain than I felt.

One more circle in the sky, and the jet bounced onto the sticky tarmac of Dacca International Airport. My heart was pounding an erratic Asian beat as I got in line for the door and the anticipated fresh sweet air of our new tropical Bengali home.

The cabin door pushed outward. I was shoved onto the top landing by the heaving queue behind me. I grabbed the railing and held on, sucking in a breath. A stench of rotting wastes whammed my senses. I stumbled down the steps and onto the melting tarred surface of my "dream of India."

People were swarming everywhere, screeching recognition as they grabbed relatives from the line of disembarking passengers. The gymnasium-sized flat roof of the airport building was jammed with waving, yelling people. The walkways overflowed with humanity.

How could they breathe through the body odors, the fumes of waste products?

Could they hear their own words above the shouts, the jangling bells, the honking, burping horns?

I forced myself not to cover my ears, but I couldn't quell the quaking of my knees. 'What have we brought on ourselves,' I thought. 'What are we doing here?'

My vision fogged. As I felt myself begin to wobble, a strong hand caught my arm. Startled, I turned to see a handsome young Bengali man looking at me with concern.

"Memsahib," he said in studied English, "I am Habib from the Ford Foundation office. Let us go quickly off this tarmac. It is too very much hot for you, I am thinking. Come."

I felt shaky and lightheaded as he led me, stumbling, into the Passenger Arrival room where whirring overhead fans pushed the wet heat into the corners and swallowed the outside noises.

"Thank you so very much, Mr. Habib. This feels far better. The heat and humidity took me by surprise. Is this where we go through Customs?" I asked, as I looked around for a sign.

My husband and sons, in a similar dazed state, were wandering around the waiting room, peering at various arrowed posters printed in Bengali, looking for "Customs."

"Not to worry, Memsahib. Customs handling is in my control. You need only to sign papers after things are declared. Your sahib and young sahibs will come with me. If you wish, you may rest in the main terminal waiting lobby." He pointed to the huge hall at the end of the walkway.

"Most new memsahibs find it of interest to people-watch."

Mr. Habib flashed me a lop-sided grin, so warm and infectious that I headed for that ocean of people without any hesitation. 'I can slip in without being noticed,' I thought, 'find a bench out of the way, and observe.'

There were no benches. No empty wall spaces. Only clusters of people crammed together. Mothers yanked their little ones closer. Husbands moved in as if to protect their families, cornering me with suspicious eyes. I smiled, hoping to appear friendly.

Almost as one, the sea of dark faces turned toward me, watchful, unsmiling.

From the nearest of the clusters, a scrawny Bengali man emerged. Sweat beads dripped from his jutting chin onto the black hairs of his chest. He sidled toward me, gaping at my short red hair and pale skin. His brow was grooved with curiosity. Knots of people gave a collective "whoosh" of breathy surprise.

I studied the ceiling.

He came closer to examine the freckles on my sleeveless arms. His eyes slid to my bosom and stayed for inspection. Voices among the clusters "waa-ed."

I stepped back, smoothed down my blouse, looked at the walls.

He edged forward, rocking sideways, staring at my body—staring, slipping closer, staring. The people gabbled.

I shifted position and searched the floor.

Garlicky fumes struck my nose. I sneezed, and took one giant step back.

Whack! The wall. No place to go. My breath came in wisps. My fingernails dug grooves into my palms.

Shaken, then indignant, I looked openly at my tormentor, and saw him for what he was—no maharajah; just a bold, curious little man, no bigger than I.

I stared directly into his startled eyes, and slid toward him.

He blinked and stepped back.

The great hall silenced.

I bent forward to examine the moist curling hairs on his narrow chest.

His black eyes bulged. He gulped and turned his attention to the walls.

Breathy "Ha's" came from the watchers.

I leaned in very close to admire the cinnamon-tinged plaid of his lungi, the skirt-like fabric which wrapped his waist and covered his hips and legs.

He choked a cough, turned and bolted into the masses from which he had come. As though on command, the clusters turned away from me, the cacophony of their voices beginning again.

With my head high, I sauntered past a wall of coldly-dismissive Bengalis. Once outside, I made a bee-line for the Customs waiting room, and the re-assurance of my family and Mr. Habib.

CHAPTER 3 **ASIAN REALITY**

As I opened the door of the Arrival/Customs building, I was greeted by my two sons. "We were just coming to look for you, Mom. Mr. Habib says that we are ready to leave the airport."

Amazed, I asked, "How did you get us and all of our luggage cleared so fast, Mr. Habib? You must be a miracle worker."

The magical Bengali with the demeanor of a New York business executive tipped his head to one side, gave us a crooked grin and said, "We Asians have our ways. Now please to follow me. Stay close. Driver will meet us by the car. My assistant will bring your luggage."

Mr. Habib elbowed a trail through the gawking crowds, who swarmed in behind us as we inched forward at his heels. The gabbling, the din, the powerful odors were beginning to overwhelm me. I was gasping and shaking by the time we reached the waiting English Ford. I plunked onto the gummy leather back seat, relieved at being out of the crowd, until I realized that the car was totally surrounded by people. I felt like a zoo animal on display, all of those brown eyes staring in, and gnarly hands pushing through the open windows.

The man behind the steering wheel turned to bob his head. "I am Driver," he said. "We go now."

He gave the horn one resounding blast, started the engine and crept the car forward to ease into the parade of vehicles leaving the airport. People surrounding the car whacked at its hot metal, their "go ahead" sign. A puff of air came through the windows—hot and acrid—but air. I grabbed in a breath, and thought, 'OK, that was just the airport. Airports are always jammed. Soon we will be at our new home, and the adventure can begin.'

Lurching ahead a wheel-turn at a time, we fell in line with the traffic crawling through the city. In front of us was a fat blue bus, painted with golden dancing ladies throwing rainbow-hued flowers. Real people sprouted from its windows, perched on its roof-top and clung to its open door. Its horn trumpeted like a rutting pachyderm, and whenever the bus sped up, we gagged on the belch of black smoke. The bus passengers pounded on its sides yelling something that must have meant "Step on it, Turtle Butt." No way could the bus driver go faster because a rickety cart piled high with straw was ahead of him in line. The water buffalo pulling the cart was not a satisfied employee. It stopped often to bellow its complaints.

A bony-chested man, carrying a baby goat around his neck, had been running along the side of the road. He stopped to beat on the water buffalo, kicking it and screaming obscenities, interesting enough for a gathering crowd to cheer him on.

I found myself being drawn into this disorganized beehive. I could almost ignore the heat, the din, the dirt, the stench. These were just people—a lot of people—going about their daily lives, hurrying to get "there," as frustrated as people in traffic jams back home.

As we approached a main boulevard, a shower of red blossoms fluttered onto the front of the car, brought down by a youngster who had climbed out onto an over-hanging tree limb. Ahead I could see a long parade of towering red-blossomed trees. Low-growing Bird-of-Paradise flowers decorated the boulevard. A great banyan tree reached out to lay its shadows on the road.

'What a beautiful tropical land we have come to,' I thought. 'It must have been exhaustion and shock from the heat that shook me so much. My fantasy, my dream of India—it really is here, waiting to be explored!'

Under the low-stretching arms of the banyan tree, a tiny woman held up her bowl to shake it at me. The piteous wail in her voice crushed my heart. Other emaciated old women sat nearby, rocking their bodies as they held up their bowls. They, too, wailed. A shirtless hunchback stepped off the road near the women. He lifted his lungi to his knees to let a steamy yellow puddle form in the hot red dust. A young mother, sitting cross-legged close by the others, casually brushed dust and urine flecks from her infant's head as she put it to breast. A howling naked toddler jumped up and down, tugging at his mother's arm. His protruding belly and coarse reddish hair told the tale of malnutrition.

I covered my eyes with my hands and sank back into the hot seat, drowning in the misery I was seeing.

'What have we done? What have we done! How can I bear this sad place?' I moaned.

My head bobbed, jerking me awake. Driver was saying, "...your street. We are almost there." I tried to shake away the haze. Had I really missed the entire ride through the city? But when the vision returned of those pathetic sights I had just seen, I was grateful for the reprieve.

We had entered a pleasant-looking residential area with tall flowering trees. But the houses all had high compound walls with barbed wire or pointed ends of broken glass jutting upwards. Dirty water ran down an open drain between the road and the wall. It had the stench of a sewer.

Our car turned onto a graveled driveway, and stopped at a closed black iron gate which had a see-through filigreed pattern. Driver honked the horn two loud toots. A small wiry man in long khaki shirt and pants, jumped out from a shady spot next to the house. He slipped into leather sandals, grabbed a lethal-looking staff, and hurried over to swing open the gate. Having completed his duty, he stood at attention, right hand to forehead.

"Driver, why is that man saluting?" I asked.

Driver waggled his head. "He used to be a military man. Now he is chowkidar. He guards the house. So he always salutes."

Sahib, also once a "military man," returned the chowkidar's salute.

The house, built of whitewashed brick, had two stories, screened wide verandahs and a covered carport. It looked beckoningly cool. But — BARS were in every window! Decorative, yes, but black metal bars.

Before I could ask about the bars, a stream of white-shirted men marched from the verandah that ran along the front of the house. They lined up in a neat row at the sidewalk's edge and salaamed as we climbed out of the car.

"Driver, who are all these people?" I asked, my apprehension growing. High compound walls; a saluting guard at the closed, metal gate; bars at the windows. Are these men here to spy on us, or to protect us from something?

CHAPTER 4   **A PROFUSION OF MALES**

"These people are your servants." Driver answered my question so curtly that I realized I had offended him. "My name is William. I am Sahib's assigned driver. Memsahib's, too, when Sahib does not require my services."

"I'm so sorry, William. I thought 'Driver' was your name."

That unintentional insult had not been a good beginning, and there was yet a long line of men to meet—the ones William had called "our servants." Would I manage to insult them all?

The world was spinning around me in humid waves of heat. I tried to smile and nod as I walked past the line-up, just managing to climb the verandah steps and into the cool house before collapsing on the lumpy cushion of a teak settee. Gratefully, I accepted a tall perspiring glass of a liquid green something. No idea what it was. It could have been grass juice, goat pee, or hemlock, whatever. It was wet, and I needed wet, so I gulped it down. Its tanginess was delicious.

"Nimbu pani [limeade], Memsahib. Good for you to feel better. Welcome to Dacca."

The sturdy-looking youngish man gave me a shy grin. "I am Kobad, Memsahib—bearer, [butler] keep house clean. Help Memsahib, Sahib, Chota Sahibs."

The remaining men whom I had seen outside were now lining up in front of us. Kobad pulled a young lad out from behind him. "Here is Hossain, Kobad helper, helps to clean in house."

Hossain's chin was almost rubbing the skin off his chest with shyness. The older man whispered to him. The boy looked up at me through long black lashes and nodded a jerky acknowledgement, immediately returning to his sleeping chicken position.

Kobad appeared clean and tidy in a long white shirt and loose pants. Hossain's T-shirt and frayed checkered lungi were soiled and rumpled. I looked around at the large, many-windowed room with its high ceilings, and thought, 'This room is spacious, but from what I have seen so far the place is no palace. Why do I need a butler? Why does the butler need a butler's helper?'

The next man to step up was surely the cook. His short white shirt stuck way out from his ample belly. I hoped we would like his cooking as well as he appeared to.

"I am Jahir Bux, pukka [very best] cook and majordomo," he stated with an outward thrust of his large chest and heavy shoulders. 'Oh my,' I thought, 'this fellow's arrogance is in full bloom.'

Jahir Bux shoved a youngster toward me. He looked to be about ten years old. "Me, Isham, cook helper," he announced in a proud little kid voice.

Isham looked even dirtier than Hossain. He was cute, with a toothy grin and wavy hair, but he would not be working in my kitchen unless he cleaned himself up! 'Besides, does the cook really need a helper?'

Mentally, I tapped these "servants" off on my fingers: driver, William; butler, Kobad; his helper, Hossain; cook and "chairman" of the servants [majordomo] Jahir Bux; his helper, Isham.

Another fellow was still in the line-up, although off to one side. He wore a frayed but clean white shirt. His lungi was a brown checkered fabric which knotted up so high on his waist that his dark knobby knees showed.

Jahir Bux jerked his head toward the young man. "He is James, Christian. Cleans floors and bathrooms. No Muslim clean those places .. in.. in," he hesitated, "in Englishman house."

James never looked up, but he shuffled his feet and nodded slightly, sliding a little farther away from the others still standing there.

As Sahib started to give a greeting speech, another lad poked his head through the door of the back verandah. He looked intently at me but waited for Kobad's introduction.

"Joseph, Christian, is mali—does garden working." Then Kobad flicked the middle finger of his right hand toward Joseph, who immediately withdrew.

"Is that everyone, Kobad?" Surely it had to be!

"Yes no, Memsahib. Chowkidar come."

Ali, the gate-keeper and night guard we had seen earlier, marched into the room and saluted Sahib, his new Commandant.

He turned sharply, cracked his dusty bare heels together and marched from the room as if he were on parade.

"Is that IT, Kobad?"

"Hahgee, Memsahib. IT!" He waggled his neck in the Asian "maybe yes, maybe no" manner, which, at the time I mistook for an assured "yes."

Before numbness set in, I decided to follow a curving stairway that led to the second floor. I found the laundry room, a bedroom-sitting room with lavatory, and a lounge area. Half of the second story had no roof. It was surrounded on three sides with a low retaining wall. The intense sun rays had charred the graveled surface of the open area so much that it made snap-crackle noises when I stepped onto it. I hurried back to the lounge room to flop onto the flowery cushions of a well-used chaise.

'Now this I could get used to,' I thought, as I lay back for a bit of jet lag repair.

Out of my mist came a voice from the stairs. "Memsahib, Kobad espeak. Dhobi come."

"All right, Kobad, bring it on, whatever it is." I laid back, eyes closed, too tired to care.

"Memsahib!" A shrill voice shaved my nerves, bringing me upright, and almost bumping noses with a tiny Bengali man, whose nose-wart hair tickled my face.

"Memsahib, Hassam here. Dhobi." The word 'dhobi' seemed to stimulate him to growth. He stood up stick-straight, chin lifted, chest expanding like an inflating balloon.

"Best wash clothes in Dacca!" He swaggered with this statement. "Wash two days your house. What two days?"

I had no idea what days. Having just arrived in Dacca, I knew nothing of the schedules. I had not even known someone else would be washing our clothes. Grasping for the memsahib reality, I threw out, "Tuesdays and Fridays should be fine."

"Memsahib!" Add harsh to shrill. "Muslims go mosque Fritys. Hassam Muslim."

"Oh, sorry, Hassam. Then you choose—except Sundays. Christians go church Sunday. Memsahib Christian."

I wasn't sure that this Muslim country allowed churches for Westerners. But I, the Memsahib, should establish something, I supposed.

"Ahcha, I come Toosty, Satidy." Pause. "Memsahib, this excellent dhobi not wash cook's dirty clothes. This dhobi not like cook."

I leaned forward, scowling, "Of course you will wash cook's uniforms! They need to be very clean because he will be preparing our food."

"Memsahib, messy cook wipe hand on apron, pant. I tell him go wash clothes in river, on rock like village woman. Good enough for him! This excellent dhobi, city man, clean man. Cook, dirty man. Bah!"

With this dissertation, "city man, clean man" carefully pulled down the loose sleeves of his snowy white kamiz-style shirt. Then he flapped the wide legs of his baggy white pants to show off their spotlessness.

"Ahcha, Memsahib. This dhobi wash cook uniforms," hesitation, side-ways glance, "in last water."

"No, Hassam! You will wash cook's uniforms with all the other white clothes, not in any dirty water."

Head down, he muttered a reluctant, "Hah-gee." Pause. "Memsahib, your washer come soon?"

"No. You will use the Foundation washing machine."

"Bah! No good machine! You buy new machine for this excellent dhobi."

I snorted. "Not likely."

"Bah! You bring press?"

"Do you mean an iron? No, I did not bring an iron. You will use..."

"Bah! Foundation press no good. You need to buy press from a memsahib who is going back to Ameriki. Ameriki press best for this excellent dhobi."

I took a deep breath and let it all out as I laid my head back on the lounge pillow. Enough of this guy! My eyes closed against a shooting pain.

Hassam's sandals whooshed on the terrazzo as he swiveled to leave.

"Toosty, Satidy. Salaam." Slide, pad, pad, slide, down the curving stairway.

Ah, at last, quiet!

"Memsahib, herman come."

'Herman? Sounds German.' Curious, I answered, "Yes, Kobad, send Herman."

Clump, clump, clump up the stairs came Herman. A tall man, half again larger than the Bengali men, stood before me. His face was covered with long black whiskers, from which peered intensely blue eyes. He wore baggy gray pantaloons and a flapping gray shirt that stretched to his knees. His head was wrapped in a blue and white striped turban, and as I looked down at his feet, I saw why he had clumped up the stairs. Enormous tire-tread sandals covered his sockless toes. This man was unlike any Bengali I had so far seen, but I hadn't seen any Germans who looked like that, either.

"How do you do, Herman? What work do you do?" I asked.

"No Ingrazi, Memsahib," he answered, as his grin developed to show stubs of rotted, red-stained teeth.

Kobad interceded. "He is babra—herman." He pulled his fingers across his own smooth face as though to shave, then pretended to cut his own short wavy hair.

"Oh! He is the barber," I laughed. "He is the HAIR man."

'Herman' nodded vigorously, then muttered an aside to Kobad.

Kobad frowned. He hesitated.

"What did he say, Kobad?" I asked.

"He say, Memsahib got fat hair. He want to know if Sahib and young Sahibs have fat hair, too. He likes fat hair, wants to cut fat hair everyone in family. Also cut face."

'Not mine, he won't!' I thought. 'I'm not comfortable with this guy. Sahib can handle him. That has got to be all the helpers. What more could possibly be necessary?'

No sooner thought than Kobad said, "Memsahib, dherzi come."

A small plump man in neatly pleated lungi and Western-style white shirt jumped in front of my chair. He must have sneaked in behind the 'babra".

"'Day, Memsahib. Estand! I weel tape you."

I hesitated, not sure I understood what he was saying.

"Estand! Estand!" he demanded in high imperious voice.

Startled, I 'estood'. He whipped out his measuring tape and headed for my bosom, which he began to prod.

He leered at me, "All memsahib like," he stated.

"OUT! NOW!" I screeched. "Kobad, get this filthy creature out of here, and never allow him in my sight again! And, please, Kobad, no more people today."

I turned my head away from the direction of the stairway and closed my eyes. 'I'm going to stay up here and rest awhile,' I thought. 'The idea of all those men around the house is unnerving to me. The "sahibs" didn't seem bothered, though. They are probably being guided around the house right now, and if I know them, they are mentally staking out their territories.'

CHAPTER 5 **TUNING IN**

I had thought that a *memsahib* was just the title given a Western woman in an Asian setting—the "little wifey" of the *sahib*, or Western man, often a leader or boss. But it appeared that I, as the *memsahib* had a job. I was supposed to manage this all-male household of servants.

How was I going to adjust to life in this foreign culture with a bunch of men running around in my house every day? These were not even people I knew. I had been raised in a family of girls, had attended an all-girls' nursing school, and had worked mostly with women in hospital settings. My children were male, of course, but that was Pediatrics, my specialty, and Mom stuff, too.

I did not feel prepared to manage an all-male household.

Many Western women, living abroad, I had been told, became restless and dissatisfied because they could not adjust to Asian ways. I could hear my own whining, knew it could happen to me. But an opportunity to live in such as exotic country was too rare and wonderful to be diminished by my own inability to cope. As it was, two years would be a very short time to begin to understand the culture and uniqueness of this tropical land and its people.

In those first days, before I became familiar with the work patterns, I was frequently shooing James away from his bathroom cleaning duties because I needed to use the room. Or chasing Kobad away from bed-making when I wanted to change clothes. I longed for privacy.

Could I even get myself a cup of tea? Oh, no. Cook would shoo me out of the kitchen with, "Kobad bring you tea now, Memsahib." I couldn't even carry my own tea up to the flat roof-top sitting room—the only peaceful place in the house, and then, only on the days the dhobi was not washing clothes.

Whine, whine—there it was again. Time for me to focus on developing management skills, which in my case probably meant non-interference, until I could figure out the dynamics of our circle of workers, their relationships to one another, and their personalities.

The term "servant" was a hang-over from the colonial British, but to my mind, it denoted slavery and I felt embarrassed by its use. These men were household employees, most of whom knew their jobs well, and were paid the customary rate. I complained about them, but at this point I couldn't do any of their jobs adequately myself. I still felt most secure when watching the street scenes from my flat-roofed eyrie.

Kobad was a comfortable man to have around the house, if one must have a butler. His manner was quiet, never intrusive. His dark brown eyes were observant without condemning. Despite his many cleaning duties, he stayed neat and fresh-looking in his loose white shirt and pants uniform. His paunch was that of a middle-aged man, though he was probably in his early thirties.

One day I asked him how old he was. "I came the year the big cyclone blew away our village."

"What year was that?"

"I don't know, Memsahib." Not an unusual reply, since villagers' important dates were noted by memories and oral histories, not by calendars.

Kobad tried his best to please us. One of the ways was to dote on the young sahib. He cleaned his room constantly, made his bed, hung up carelessly dumped clothes, dusted and preened Steve's desk, even polished his bike!

Finally, Memsahib Mom said, "No more! When Steve goes back to America, he will not have a butler to fulfill his every need. He has to learn to take care of himself. You can help out if things get too messy; otherwise, leave it up to him."

It was hard for Kobad to let go of that, but he found other ways to ensure his job.

Our shoes were always dusty during the dry season, and wet and muddy in monsoon time. Kobad asked us to leave our grubby shoes

Never Cheat A Holy Man

outside the bedroom door at night so he could pick them up to clean, and return in the morning when he brought our coffee.

One such morning Kobad commented on the hole in the toe of one of my most comfortable pairs of soft leather shoes.

"Memsahib, my friend very good shoemaker. Make you perfect new shoes, good price."

Since those shoes were not going to be wearable much longer, and the local Bata Shoes store catered to the floppy sandals clientele, I decided to give his friend a try.

"All right, Kobad, but please tell your friend that Memsahib wants the new shoes to be just like the old ones."

Kobad assured me they would be.

The next week, Kobad brought me a newspaper-wrapped package. His eyes were downcast, his chin pushing his chest.

"Memsahib's perfect shoes," he stated, without looking up at me.

He had been right. The shoemaker had made the shoes "just like the old ones," as I had requested—including the hole in the toe.

Hossain, Kobad's young helper, was like an apparition, always behind Kobad, watching and repeating Kobad's movements. He was silent except for the sound of his large bare feet as they hit against the terrazzo floor—flap, flap, flap—like waves against a rocky shore. Kobad was a patient teacher, and the boy practiced his tasks with growing confidence. He learned to change the sheets, make the beds, dust the settee and plump up its pillows. Kobad gave him more complicated tasks as he showed his understanding.

One morning Hossain and Kobad came to stand before me, a pathetic-looking duo. Kobad's face was a storm cloud, and Hossain's downcast eyes dripped with moisture. Kobad dug his elbow into the weeping boy's arm.

"Make bad mistake, Memsahib," Hossain stuttered. "Kobad say shake out pillows." He pointed to the clothes-line on the back verandah. The empty pillow covers drooped over the lines. The breeze scuttled fluffy white feathers into billowy clouds. The terrazzo was snowy with pillow entrails. Hossain had opened the inner cases to shake out the pillows. Isn't that what Kobad had said?

Poor Hossain, mortified by his mistake, was also fearful of losing his job. He was just a skinny village kid, hardly older than my youngest son. He had probably never seen the inside of a Memsahib house before. His village home would be made of bamboo and mud; his bed, a cot made of rope. Pillows like ours? Not likely.

I wanted so much to give him a hug and tell him it was okay, but I had vowed not to interfere. Kobad was a firm guide and mentor, and did not need intervention from me. Hossain stayed on the job, and if he ever made another mistake, I didn't hear about it.

Hassam, the pain-in-the-neck dhobi, came to wash and iron for our household the agreed-upon two days a week. I was tempted to sack him (as the British say) because of his demanding ways, but when I mentioned this to friends, they began to bicker over who would get him to work for them. They admitted having tried, but he was already working six days a week. He was very annoying, often upsetting the entire household, but I did admire his efficiency.

He washed the clothes for Sahib and me, and for the young sahibs; also, our linens and the uniforms for the indoor servants. He hung them on the flat-roof clothes-lines to dry enough to get the ironing started, which he finished before he left for the day.

"Thank you, Hassam, for your hard work," I often told the dhobi. "I know that the cook makes more work for you, but when you scold him too much about his messiness he just gets more obstinate." My comments did not stop their noisy little battles one bit.

One day I heard the high rasping voice of Hassam coming from the kitchen, with an equally unpleasant throat-grating reply.

"What is going on here?" I demanded. Non-interference be damned; this was ridiculous.

Hassam was waving one of Jahir Bux's grease-stained aprons full in the cook's face. Jahir Bux, half again bigger than Hassam, was grabbing at both the apron and the tiny dhobi, ready for a shake-shake. The two men stopped in mid-bellows when I entered, but immediately began to jabber at me, stating their positions. Crescendos rose. Arms chopped the air.

"Estop!" I scolded, trying to raise my voice above theirs. "You two are behaving like children. You will work out your problems, or Sahib will take disCIPlinary action, (British version). Settle this right now. I will be in the living room. You will come and tell me what arrangements you have made." Head high, this decisive Memsahib stomped from the kitchen.

The wrangling continued but with fewer outbursts until, finally, the two proud men marched into the living room to stand before me.

"And what is your agreement?" I asked, still expecting another outbreak.

"This dirty cook agrees to wipe his hands on clean rags and not on his apron, pant or shirt," Hassam stated, his entire body quivering with superiority. "And he will also prepare my lunch. All other cooks do that, Memsahib, but he has refused to do so in the past. NOW, he shall do!" Diminutive, squeaky-voiced Hassam had triumphed.

"Jahir Bux, are you willing to cooperate with Hassam? What will Hassam do for you?" I did not believe for one minute that Jahir Bux would not turn this deal to his own advantage.

"This buzzing mosquito of a dhobi will be washing my uniforms with first whites, after Sahib's. And he will be starching and pressing them properly, not sloppy like before."

He turned to leer at Hassam as he continued, "And he will be washing my lungis when he washes his own," he rolled his eyes slyly toward me, "in your water, Memsahib, using your soap, Memsahib. Did you know that, Memsahib?"

Of course, Jahir Bux was telling tales on Hassam. In his mind, Hassam's use of Memsahib's washing equipment and soap was devious, unless his own personal things could be washed, too.

Calm had been restored to the household. Maybe I was catching on.

Late afternoon on the next laundry day, I entered the dining room to be greeted with a hurricane of protest by cook, dhobi, AND butler.

The clean laundry of the day was stacked in neat piles on the banquet-sized dining room table. Hanging from the overhead chandelier were Jahir Bux's uniforms, almost glistening in their purity of whiteness—and so stiffly starched that, had they jumped off their hangers they could have marched away.

"Hassam!" I said, in my sternest Memsahib voice. "What does this mean?"

Jahir Bux butted in to answer before Hassam's squeaky words could get out.

"Memsahib, this ungrateful creature threw lunch box at me. Poison, he say. Bah!"

Hassam began to jump up and down, screeching, "Hassam is good Muslim. Not eat food cooked in ghee of infidels. Cook say he is best Muslim, say he pray five times a day, but, Lazy Man, he sleep instead, Memsahib. Did you know that, Memsahib? And he eats food he cooks for Sahib, who is not Muslim. Did you know that is what he is doing, Memsahib? Our Koran forbids this. Cook no good Muslim!"

"Hassam, you will take these uniforms back upstairs and re-wash them. NOW! You, Jahir Bux, will prepare a meal that you know Hassam can eat. If you do not do so from this time forward, Sahib will lower your pay and give the difference to Hassam."

Now Kobad edged closer, dark eyes hang-dogging me.

"All right, Kobad, what is your problem here?"

"Memsahib, cook not let me do my job to put clean clothes away. Say Memsahib must see. Jahir Bux push me! Dhobi push me, too! I do not fight, only want to do my work for Sahib and Memsahib." Kobad's face was ruddy red as tears dribbled down his cheeks.

I assured my gentle bearer that everything would be all right now ...I hoped.

Management-wise, Jahir Bux was my biggest problem. He couldn't just be ignored, because I had to interact with him about our food likes and dislikes, and to see that the many sanitation rules were followed exactly. Our water had to be boiled for twenty minutes; our vegetables had to be soaked in disinfectant; all food had to be thoroughly cooked.

Jahir Bux hated that I, a mere woman, gave him instructions and checked that they were followed carefully. At first when I asked him to try certain new recipes, he ignored me. But if I told him that "Sahib liked," he listened.

One morning, I went into the kitchen to show him how to cook a rice recipe the American way that would please Sahib. I went over it with him one time, then asked if he had understood.

"Hahgee, Memsahib. I know. You go now." He turned to face me. "Too many cooks in this kitchen!"

I felt the rise of blood to my face. My head pounded. "Jahir Bux!" I screeched like an Irish fish monger, "Whose kitchen do you think this is?"

That miserable cook thumped his puffed-out chest with his fat fist. "My kitchen, Memsahib! My kitchen!" As far as he was concerned, he would always rule the kitchen.

I stomped out of his kitchen caught between anger and laughter. Until then, I had actually believed that I, the Memsahib of the New Management, was in charge.

CHAPTER 6 **RUBBISH GIVERS; RUBBISH REMOVERS**

Joseph, the gardener, worked mostly in the cooler early morning hours, trying to keep the tropical greenery from pushing the house off the property. The compound was about an acre in size with six-foot white-washed brick walls all the way around. If anyone needed to have a helper it seemed to me that Joseph should have been the one, but he had no rank in society, except that of Christian. In this largely Muslim country, that did not count for much.

He was a steady worker, reasonably efficient, but he could not get vegetables to grow. Sahib gave him vegetable seeds and showed him how to lay out a special garden for them. Joseph was delighted, waiting eagerly for the new plants to pop through. But as soon as the little green shoots showed up, so did the little green bugs, the fat brown worms, and the hungry mynah birds. Poor Joseph, unable to contend, apologized constantly.

One day he shyly presented Sahib with a handful of foot-length green beans. He didn't outright say he had grown them, but the implication was that he might have. We knew they had come from the greenhouse of our neighbor, who was a long-term resident. Joseph wanted a greenhouse, too. Good promotional gimmick that his bean gift was, since our property was a rental, we weren't free to do that for him. He was stuck with flower gardening and weed bashing, and we stayed with iodine-soaked, over-cooked vegetables from the market, or boring, but safe canned ones.

In our household Jahir Bux, was responsible for overseeing the household, as well as being the cook. The other servants knew they were to go to him with questions and problems. Then he was to decide what was important enough to be brought to the attention of Sahib. When Jahir Bux went on leave, Kobad fulfilled that duty.

I was in "Jahir Bux's" kitchen one morning while he was away at his village and Kobad was out shopping, when I heard angry yelling in the back garden. The most likely perpetrators were the cook and the dhobi, but since neither man was here, who was causing the ruckus?

I stepped outside my back verandah in time to catch mild-mannered Joseph slinging garbage and tin cans at some gray-bearded fellow I had never seen before. Gray-beard was standing next to a garbage pile of his own, from which he picked choice missiles to heave at Joseph. Vendetta sailed through the air with the articles they pitched.

This was looking too dangerous to be allowed to come to its own conclusion. It was time to run interference.

"Estop!" I demanded, stepping between the two men. A rotten onion, already in mid-air struck my cheek. Joseph and Gray-beard came running to me, mortification in their fawning bows. They babbled, clasped their palms and rocked their bodies in front of me. 'Now what should I do?' I thought. 'I can't communicate well enough to work this out.'

Just in time, Kobad appeared, like a genie from his lamp. He dropped his shopping bag on the verandah step and marched over to the two gardeners. With calm firmness he questioned the men in the Bengali language they could understand.

The problem had started when Jahir Bux (wouldn't you know!) had given Joseph the non-burnable garbage to toss out.

"I ask where to put garbage, but Cook no say, just flip head toward back wall. So that is where I chuck it," Joseph explained, as he pointed to high brick wall at the back of the property.

Graybeard's face shone red, even through his whiskers. He, the mali of the house on the other side of the wall, had been roundly chastised by his Sahib for having accrued such a mess. Humiliated and furious, he had collected that trash, added his own, and was returning the lot to Joseph.

"Joseph," I said, in as calm and un-laughing a voice as I could manage, "Please apologize to this mali and promise him you will never give him our garbage again."

Kobad directed the two contrite men to pick up their mess, and carry all of it to a heap on the outside of our west wall, a dump site already high with other neighbors' waste deposits.

I followed along to assure myself that our garbage was properly deposited. When a fat-bellied rat ran out of the dump, barely missing my foot, I said, "Kobad, when will this disgusting stuff be picked up?"

I was thinking 'garbage truck schedule,' and I hoped it would be imminent.

"Rubbish pickers just now coming, Memsahib," Kobad responded, pointing to a bald-necked vulture that flapped down onto the middle of the heap. The repulsive bird hissed as it poked its long beak into the newest dump of trash.

Several more of the huge birds soon flopped onto the mess, amid much ungainly flapping and noisy squawking. These birds were uglier than garbage trucks, smelled about the same, but were more efficient, because they didn't haul to yet another dump site. Much of this stuff would be picked over, dragged off or decayed by morning...Pakistan's disposal system.

These waste sites also fed starving widows, orphaned children, mangy homeless pariah dogs. This was the flip side of a beautiful tropical country where there was not enough food nor enough land for one of the largest populations per square mile in the world.

As I looked at this stinking heap, I thought about those who were seeking the barest existence from my own wastefulness. I turned away in shame, feeling heavy with helplessness.

CHAPTER 7 **ONE COOL CHICKEN**

Dawn brought another blistering day, the sun already at melting point. I stepped from the verandah into the back garden just as Jahir Bux came riding up to the kitchen door on his rickety green bicycle. He had already been to market to buy the freshest produce before it turned into vulture fodder.

"Salaam, Memsahib," he greeted me cheerily. "Buy *pukka* chicken for tonight's dinner. You see?"

He would not have needed to point out his "excellent" poultry selection. The wretched bird, its feet tied together, had been slung upside down over the handlebars. It was flapping its wings and squawking in frantic protest.

"Jahir Bux, please take that poor creature out of the sun. And be sure to let it cool well before you prepare it for dinner." My grandmother had taught me about cooling fresh chicken meat before cooking it.

Jahir Bux rolled his dark eyes upward to meet the shaggy eyebrows as he frowned, but he "*bahgee'd*" his Asian assent. He waggled his head as he slung the complaining fowl over his shoulder to carry into the house.

I called to him as he headed for the kitchen, "Why don't you make chicken curry for Sahib tonight? You haven't made any for us yet. I'm sure it would be very good."

A low growl came from deep in his throat. I heard him slap the chicken onto the cement counter top, after which he glared out at me from the kitchen door, and shouted, "Memsahib, this pukka cook does not make *kari*. Only village woman make *kari*!"

I must remember to not ever ask this cook to make "*kari*." Allah forbid he would do a woman's job! I'm betting it's too hard for him...all that grinding of spices to blend into the perfect subtle flavors so prized by connoisseurs of Asian cuisine.

It took much restraint not to yell back, "Betcha can't even do it!"

Every day after morning work was completed, and the family had finished lunch, Jahir Bux and the other workers went to their quarters at the back of the compound to eat their lunches and take afternoon rest. Because of the intense mid-day heat, work came to a halt everywhere in the city between the hours of 1:00 p.m. and 4:00 p.m. This was the quietest time of day—or night. What didn't get done during the daylight hours was worked on in the cool of the night. All night, loudly!

The long afternoon rest was a tradition of the culture, and although our house was partially air-conditioned, which would have made it comfortable for the servants to finish their work earlier, I liked the tradition. Everyone was out of my hair. It was quiet, inside and out. No job seekers came pounding at the door, offering glowing self-written chits about their prowess as servants; no newspaper *wallahs* passing on the road, screeching "*Ikagosh! Ikagosh!*"as they tried to sell their papers. Even the high nasal intoning of the mullah calling the Muslim faithful to prayer was silent during these hours. I could write and think without interruption. This was my time to NOT be a Memsahib.

This particular day, I sat at the dining room table to catch up on letter writing, but found my thoughts being disrupted by a scratch-scratch noise. It sounded like a mouse or rat but I couldn't tell where it was scratching.

The search began. I listened along the dining room walls, moved slowly through the swinging door and along the hallway that led to the screened back verandah, and into the kitchen. Aha! definitely louder in the kitchen. With suspicious caution, I peeked behind the kettles stacked on the lower shelves, looked into the dish pan sitting in the cement sink. *SCRITCH! SCRITCH!* I poked a long knife under the decrepit kerosene stove. Nothing ratty ran out.

Then—*SCRITCH! SCRITCH!* Oh, I just knew it. Some big Mama Rat was making her nest under the refrigerator. The scratching was right in there! For the first time, I actually wished that Jahir Bux was in my—no, his—kitchen to confront the varmint. I leaned against the refrigerator door to consider my options. Thump, thump, thump against my back.

Not having the sense Allah gave a chicken, I yanked open the refrigerator door.

"BRUK *bruk, bruk, bru u u u u uk* BRUK BRUK."

Out jumped my chicken dinner, feathers intact, flapping and squawking that it was chilled quite enough, thank you!

CHAPTER 8 **COLD TOAST AND HOT TEA**

Perhaps Jahir Bux deserved the benefit of the doubt this time. He might not have understood my request to cool the chicken. However, I was not so naive as to think he would never try to sabotage the Memsahib if he could get away with it.

The food we were served laid heavy on our spoiled American stomachs. I had shown Jahir Bux several new recipes but he had taken my suggestions as an insult, stubbornly continuing to serve greasy fried eggplant, slimy okra and rubbery long green beans. White rice, often including tiny stones or beetle parts, came with most meals. The chicken took up a lot of dinner time while we removed its stringy bits from our teeth. Beef didn't get into our teeth, though. It just bounced.

Not the cook's fault, that. Unlike American beef, which ages after death, Pakistani beef aged on the hoof, since cattle were not supposed to be killed to eat until they had no other useful function. Occasionally, butchering took place at roadside on the walk to market because the cow had collapsed on the way.

The fresh local fruits, such as bananas and papayas, sustained us the best. These did not have to be soaked in iodine or cooked before eating because their contaminated outer coverings could be peeled and discarded.

We tried not to complain, knowing that the local people had to eat this same type of food, and would feel blessed if they could have, in one week, what we had in one meal. Besides, this was only a temporary discomfort for us. Three months before we left the States, I had ordered a six-month supply of food from a warehouse in

Denmark. The Pakistani government gave us that privilege, duty-free, to keep us from draining down the limited local food supply. We had been warned that the order would take five or six months to reach us because the Chittagong, East Pakistan port was just one of many unloading locations around the world.

We could wait it out, of course, but one thing that really bugged us, something I felt was fixable, was the cold toast we were served at breakfast. Jahir Bux had worked for a British family before being assigned to us. Cold toast was liked by the Brits, we had been told. Not by Americans. Not these Americans, anyway. We had not yet found a toaster to buy here so the kerosene burner had to suffice, camp-stove style.

So far I had been avoiding this issue because of my attempt at the non-confrontational approach. Or was it intimidation?

Our household was still settling in when Habib phoned from the local General Service Office. "Eight international V.I.P. ladies are coming to Dacca tomorrow. You will please to entertain them for late afternoon tea?"

He was very polite, but clearly his question was a statement, not a request. One of my duties as the wife of a Ford Foundation advisor in an isolated area like East Pakistan was to entertain foreign visitors and personnel. Because Dacca had no suitable Western-style hotel, our General Service Office maintained a small guest house. Any over-flow visitors were farmed out to Ford Foundation families. Thus the need for large houses and numerous servants.

I choked, "Yes, of course, Habib. Tomorrow afternoon then, it will be."

Oh, Lordy, Lordy, what was I thinking? I dropped the phone into its cradle, and yelled.

"Jahir Bux! Jahir Bux! I need you!" (Did I actually say that?) I bent over, rocking, rubbing at my throbbing head.

Jahir Bux came tromping through the swinging dining room door, making blotchy chicken-blood handprints on his freshly-starched white apron as he ran. His eyes were crinkled in question, maybe even concern.

"What am I going to do, Jahir Bux? Habib says I am to entertain eight ladies from overseas… tomorrow, Jahir Bux, tomorrow! I am not ready. We don't have enough dishes. I have no idea what we can serve them." My voice rose to a wail, trailing to a sob.

Relief spread over Jahir Bux's round face like soft ghee on warm bread. "Not to worry, Memsahib. This pukka cook will serve perfect tea. Memsahib go to Foundation office, borrow dishes. Warehouse has everything you need. Memsahib ask Habib Sahib. No problem."

For once his "yes, no, maybe" Asian head-waggling gave me confidence. He was managing me, and I was grateful.

Tomorrow became today. Kobad and Hossain were whirling dervishes, setting up small tables, adding borrowed chairs and linens, preparing plates and silverware. Cleaning, cleaning, cleaning. Joseph came to the back verandah door loaded with greens and flowers.

"Joseph, thank you. These are lovely. Where did you get them? Are they from our garden?" I had not seen such luscious red blossoms anywhere around our compound.

Joseph's brown face took on a ruddy glow. "No, Memsahib, green house mali send flowers for Memsahib's tea party."

Impressive! But how did he know about the tea party unless Joseph had told him? Made me wonder if all the servants gossiped about the goings-on in their employers' homes. Hmm, something to remember.

I glanced nervously out the front window, thinking about the guest arrivals. Ali, the gatekeeper and chowkidar, wearing a stiff new khaki uniform, was practicing one of his imagined duties of marching back and forth in front of the latticed iron gate. He tapped the ground and whacked noisily at the gate with his night-stick as he swung along. Marijan, the neighbors' chowkidar, was standing in the middle of the road. Big, tough Marijan loved to bully scrawny-boned Ali.

'That had better not be going on now,' I thought.

I opened the door a crack, and caught the tones of Marijan's booming Pathan voice singing a marching song to help Ali keep cadency. Fantastic! Everyone, even Marijan, was getting into the act.

Oh! But what about Jahir Bux? The most important part, and I had forgotten all about it! I dashed through the hallway, into the living room, into the dining room, through the swinging door, into the verandah hallway, lurching and breathless, through the kitchen entrance.

"Memsahib, *OUT!*"

I slid back out the door. This was no time for either one of us to get our tails in a twist. The other fellows were doing everything right.

I would just have to have faith that my *"pukka"* cook would do the same.

I showered and changed to calm myself before the guests arrived. Promptly at 4:00 p.m., the eight lovely ladies skipped onto the front verandah, laughing to each other about the salutes they had been given by Ali and Marijan. These women were wives of agricultural scientists who were attending an international meeting in Dacca. Conversation flowed easily because they all spoke English, despite representing various Asian and European countries.

Kobad came to whisper in my ear. "Do you wish for the food to be served now? Jahir Bux is needing to know."

"Yes, please, Kobad, whenever it is ready."

"Ladies," I said, "Kobad tells me tea is about to be served. I hope you will enjoy it."

I wanted to tell them that they had better hope for the best. I was! But I didn't want them to get up and leave, so I just grinned a "good hostess" smile, and crossed my fingers.

When Habib had requested the afternoon tea party, I was thinking of the casual American afternoon tea—little sandwiches and a few nice cookies with tea or coffee. I should have remembered that Jahir Bux had been trained to the ways of the British, who served a much more formal and filling "high tea" in late afternoon.

The food came—and came—and came: refreshing chilled mango fruit soup; green banana fried chips, more tender and crispy than any potato chips I had ever tasted; an eggplant sambal with a lively tang of hot peppers; crispy little rice pappadams that crunched into airy flavor when chewed; *AND* large succulent prawns with a delicately spiced curry dip.

All of this was served with sweet Pakistani chai, heavy with boiled buffalo milk.

The ladies munched and crunched and raved. "Where has all this wonderful food come from? How did you find this marvelous cook?" On and on.

Shamelessly I waved it off with, "Oh, this is just local Pakistani fare," as though I weren't just as astounded as they were. Now that I had seen Jahir Bux's true capabilities he wasn't getting away with any more lousy meals.

As we were eating, I caught glimpses of Jahir Bux on the back verandah, peeking in through the windows to measure our delight.

We had just licked up the last crumbs and were sitting back to digest, when we heard a soft "Ho, Memsahib" at the dining room doorway. In waltzed Jahir Bux. On his right hand was balanced a silver platter, displaying a beautiful yellow cake decorated in fluted white icing.

He swept it down in front of each guest in turn for her to read.

HAPI WELCUM
LADI-FRUTES
CAKE

Every LADI clapped, and not one LADI laughed. It was a delicious lemon cake with bits of papaya and pineapple in it. I was awed, especially considering the unreliable state of my kerosene stove's oven. Jahir Bux eventually admitted that he had bribed the neighbor's cook, whose memsahib had an American stove with a working oven.

The tea party had been a delightful success, largely due to the enthusiasm of all of the servants. And especially, Jahir Bux. As expected, he strutted about in peacock pride. And being on the ultimate high of himself, he was very approachable...the perfect time to bring up that annoying little problem of cold toast.

"Jahir Bux," I said, after I had congratulated him many, many times on the fine tea he had prepared, "Sahib has requested me to ask if you could serve our toast warm instead of cold. We Americans are funny that way. We prefer warm toast."

"Hahgee, Memsahib, I weel do my best." Never before had I heard such an agreeable answer from Jahir Bux.

I was beginning to see that the way to handle this domineering male was to give him special entertainment challenges. The more kudos he got, the more cooperative he would be about mundane things.

The morning after the warm toast request, our longed-for moist, soft warm toast appeared at the breakfast table. When I asked Jahir Bux how he had managed it, what with having to use the open kerosene burner as a toaster, he just waggled his head and went back to the kitchen.

The next day I peeked in while he was making breakfast. He was using a fork to stab a piece of bread, which he held over the open flame, turning it over and over until it was golden brown.

With a quick flip, he inserted the hot toast...into the sweaty pit of his fat arm to keep warm while the next piece toasted.

The British were smarter than I had thought.

CHAPTER 9   EAST PAKISTAN HINDU FAIR

The first weeks we were in Dacca, I often went up to the flat-roofed sunroom to watch the passing parade of humanity outside our compound walls, hesitant to be a part of the scene, not knowing how to connect.

One morning I saw a grotesquely crippled old man hobble by, scraggly white head bowed, body skewed toward the wooden peg that was his leg. It left dimples in the red dust as he clumped forward. Behind him, riding the wobbly, bent frame of a bicycle, a paperboy was hollering *"Ik-agosh! Ik-agosh!,"* as he hawked his papers. He veered toward the old man, ding-dinging his bike's rusty bell, barely missing him as he headed back for his own side of the road. The crippled man crumpled into a heap, shaking his head and rubbing the ankle of his good leg as the boy rode away, his coarse mean laugh tearing into my heart. I just sat there in my cushiony chair, on the shady sunroom deck of my cool, protected, comfortable home—and bawled.

That was how Kobad, my ever-constant, thoughtful bearer found me.

"Sorry for interrupt, Memsahib. Telephone message for you." He hesitated. "Memsahib, you need me to help you? You maybe sick? I bring you nimbu pani." (His cure for everything, limeade).

"Thank you so much. I am not sick. I am just very sad. Doesn't anybody in the city feel happy? Everywhere I look I see all this poverty and disease. I have so much and others have so little. It makes me feel ashamed and helpless. I long to know that there are people in this land who are content with their lives. Are there such people?"

Kobad stood silent before me, chin on his white shirt front. Suddenly his head came up, his rounded shoulders came out of their slump and he smiled his toothy best.

"This bearer is happy, Memsahib. Cook happy, too. Village people happy. You need to see village people." He nodded his head vigorously. "I take you to Hindu mela, a country fair. You will see happy people there. *Hah-gee*, Memsahib, this you will like."

Kobad's advice had been wise. He had said to get out among the local people in a rural setting. So he and I had hopped into rickshas, whose drivers knew where to find the best little fair put on by Hindu villagers. It was just outside of teeming, stinking Dacca. As we left the city I began to smell the sweet fragrance of frangipani blossoms, not open sewers. Many small patches of rice paddies were on either side of the road. Ahead I could see a large meadow where many people were setting up their wares on boxes or cloths laid out on the ground. They were laughing and enjoying themselves. I could hear the tattoo beat of drums in the distance, and flutes wailing the tunes that enticed cobras from their baskets. The feeling of fun and excitement in the air was very like any country fair in America

True, the language was different. The wares were different...I had never seen huge clay water pots or great mounds of green pulses, ground red peppers, or yellow cumin for curries at our fairs, but chickens were pecking about and sheep and goats grazed nearby, waiting for auction.

In my excitement I called out to no one in particular, "Oh, look! There is even a game of ring-toss and a funny old push-type merry-go-round!"

The driver of my shaky bicycle ricksha turned around to give The Look that said, "Another crazy foreign memsahib."

He jangled his rusty bell, trying to shoo away a gang of little boys who were daring each other to jump in front of us. Finally he gave up, jammed on his bicycle brakes, and glared at me to get out. But the kids clustered so closely I could barely take that necessary step down.

I had another problem, too. In order not to look conspicuous, I had decided to wear a sari to the fair. But I should have had more sari-donning lessons, because this gown felt too loose. Not trusting it,

I tucked it in the best I could before I jumped. The minute I touched the ground, I was engulfed in sweaty bare-chested youngsters with loud voices and pushy ways. They pummeled each other as they pulled at me.

"Come, Memsahib, come my stall."

"No, mine. Mine! Mine!" Their screaming high-pitched voices, demanded my attention.

Little ruffians that they were, they dragged me from place to place, not giving me time to look at the wares or even to check out the gaily painted clay pots.

These kids were cute and funny, like kids anywhere, but they were beginning to frustrate me, and no one was coming to my rescue. Where had Kobad disappeared?

"Hey!" I scolded, "Stop! I want to see."

I grabbed onto the countertop of a wooden box stall, hanging on tightly while I bent low to examine some unusually long, shiny red peppers.

"Ka-choo! Ka-choo!" I sneezed and sneezed as the pungent aromas tickled my nose. The little boys went crazy, jumping up and down, choking with guffaws at the funny memsahib. They squirmed in around me so that I could hardly breathe.

My blood rose dangerously far from the patience level, and I started to push them out of the way. One skinny little guy glued himself to my waist like a blood sucker. I unclamped him, roughly shoving him off. As determined as I was to remove him, so was his determination to hang on.

He grabbed again, this time pulling at my sari's skirt. I felt the release of fabric from my waist as yards and yards of filmy blue cotton began to slide toward my ankles.

All I could think of was that every attendee at this mela was watching my mortification; that right here in front of God and Allah and Krishna I was being denuded.

The Hindu culture does not obsess about modesty in the way that the Muslim culture does. Muslim men are embarrassed to openly look at women. Hindus are earthy folks, taking a far different view—and as much as possible. I was guessing that the men here would be gathering around for the sideshow. Kobad, Muslim, would not be coming to my aid.

My face was on fire. I bent over to pull up around me as much of this twisted mess of cloth as I could, but my hands shook so hard that I could barely hang on to it. Too embarrassed to stand, I stayed down until I got dizzy. When finally I stood up to re-wrap, I noticed that none of the kids were around, but village women were beginning to encircle me. They were not smiling. They were not speaking. They were just watching me.

Had I crossed some taboo line? Had I angered the mothers of the little darlings who had pushed me around, and caused me such humiliation? I had given them some rather hard shoves!

I nodded my head at them and smiled as brightly as my precarious situation, whatever it was, would allow. It was as though I had pressed a turn-on button. They all began to talk and to touch my sari, apparently trying to explain its mysteries. Finally a well-padded mother-type stepped to my rescue. She spun me around as though she was unstringing a top, until I was almost uncovered, and the fabric was at the end of its five and one-half yards. Then she re-wound me as she smoothed, folded and pleated, finally tucking this voluminous fabric into my waist and back over my shoulder. She accomplished it with such skill that the sari felt secure and almost comfortable. The ladies murmured their approval, smiling and nodding.

I kept repeating, *"Donabad! Donabad!,"* my thanks in the only appropriate Bengali word I knew. They grinned and chattered, seeming pleased to have helped me. Mother-type took my arm to show me what the ladies were selling in their stalls. Except for babies and toddlers, the children were playing elsewhere, and the men had turned their backs, ignoring our cluster of women.

Each of the stalls sold different types of items, and I tried to show my appreciation by buying at least one thing from every lady's place: a voluptuous brass Hindu goddess; a red clay oil lamp with a flutey handle; a hand-embroidered scarf; generous packets of cardamoms and fenugreek for the curry I was probably never going to get Jahir Bux to make; and a wonderful heavy, old brass pot to use in my Japanese ikabana lessons. It seemed to be the perfect base for that type of floral display.

All too soon my bag was full and my purse was empty.

I said my "namoshkar's," my goodbyes, to the ladies, and wandered on to find Kobad. A large group of men and boys were tossing hemp-rope rings on to wall pegs. Looked simple enough until I realized that the pegs were made to sag, the trick being to hook the ring so firmly against the wall that the ring couldn't slide off even if the peg did sag. The prize was a gaudy foot-high orange and black clay elephant, but nobody won it while I was watching. It looked like a scam to me, but the gamblers were laughing and throwing their meager coins again and again. I wondered how many fairs that same prize elephant had seen.

Over by the merry-go-round, I saw my nemeses, the wild little boys, and young girls, too, holding on to toddlers as they swung round and round. A few babies screamed in panic but most of the youngsters were yelling and laughing. This is how it ought to be! I felt happier and lighter than since I had left America.

Kobad had shown me that even in their poverty, these Bengalis were happy. Their contentment lay in the joy of small things. I was profoundly impressed with the women and their rescue efforts at my dilemma. When they had realized my distress they had shooed away the kids, and had protected me from the prying eyes of the men. Probably it was a custom born of their women's need for privacy—this in a land of more than 2,000 people per square mile. I was a lucky recipient of this blessing.

The sun was lowering into the evening sky. The stall keepers were packing their wares. I wandered over to see the puny chickens that pecked relentlessly at imagined fat bugs. Kobad found me back at the ring toss, elephant prize still in display mode.

"You like mela, Memsahib?" I knew he would not mention the sari incident. He was Muslim.

"Yes, Kobad, I liked very much. Thank you for bringing me to this place where people are happy. I bought some interesting things, too. Look at this heavy old brass vase," I said, lifting it out of my bag.

He gingerly touched the rim and bent to sniff it. "Uh, Memsahib," he laughed, "this is not a vase. What for you want a spittoon?"

CHAPTER 10 **NEVER CHEAT A HOLY MAN**

Kobad took my full bag and hurried off to find the rickshas and their drivers who would be returning us to Dacca. I lingered for a few minutes to absorb the ambience of this pleasant rural scene.

"Ho, Memsahib! Ho!" Not having seen any other memsahibs at the fair, I looked around to see who was calling me.

The voice had come from the direction of an enormous banyan tree at the far corner of the compound where the fair was held. I could see a bony white cow, lounging in the shade, content with her cud. Above her, on a slanting branch, sat a strange-looking little man. When he saw that I had turned in his direction, he slid from the branch, landing in a cross-legged position.

'What is he—a leprechaun?' I thought. 'I never saw anyone do that before!'

The dung-plastered hair, the burnished leathery bare chest, and the long string of yellow beads, told me that he was a *sadhu*, a holy man. I'd never been that close to a Hindu holy man before so I moved closer for a look. He jumped straight up from his lotus position, and I saw that he was wearing nothing but a dirty white strip of cloth, which wrapped his waist, went down between his legs and back up again. He was so skinny, so angular, his eyes so constantly shifting that he scared me.

I began to back away, readying to run, but he lunged forward to grab my arm with long dirty nails that dug into my flesh.

"Come now, Memsahib. I give you blessings," He pulled me over to a pail of milk, set next to the cow. Unlike his body language, his voice was gentle, soothing even.

'He *IS* a holy man,' I thought. 'A blessing in any man's religion is probably a good thing. I'll be all right.' I stopped resisting. He released his grip.

"Memsahib want big blessing? Small blessing?" he asked, leaning in close to my face.

"Any blessing size would be fine, thank you," I said, praying that my blessing would come in the guise of Kobad.

The sadhu dipped his hand into the milk bucket and began to sprinkle "holy milk" onto the ovate leaves of the branches he could reach. As he shook off the milk, his voice rose and fell in a sing-song chant that sounded like an ancient magic incantation. He continued all around the tree, dipping, shaking and chanting, until I felt over-full from his blessings.

Slowly I backed away, calling my thanks softly, not wanting to disturb his concentration.

"*HO! MEMSAHIB!*"

'A very loud voice for such a little man,' I thought.

He reached toward me, his arm fully outstretched, palm upright and shaking.

'Oh! I'm supposed to pay for these blessings, and of course, they were the full dose. But I spent all of my money at the ladies' stalls. Kobad has the bag with things I bought, so I can't even give this fellow a gift.'

In desperation, I clawed through my little coin purse, just in case. Ah! One tiny coin was caught in a seam. It was a pai, the equivalent of one tenth of a penny.

I dropped it into his open hand. "Sorry. It's all I have left."

His mouth flew open, his eyes pinned me at dagger point. He threw down the coin, spat on it, grinding it into the dust with his crusty bare foot. He began to mutter something that was surely profane as he turned his back on me and marched over to the tree.

I hurried off as fast as I could go in my swaddling of sari. The sound of his high chant, loud and angry, followed me across the meadow. Now that I was safely away, I dared to turn for one last look.

He was wiping off my "holy blessings", and re-endowing the leaves with new incantations.

Kobad and I were probably lucky to have made it home safely.

CHAPTER 11 MODHU, RIKI TIKI TAVI of BENGAL

Young Sahib was beginning to nag me about getting the mongoose we had promised him before coming to Pakistan. I had to admit that we had not searched very hard. So one day I asked Jahir Bux if he could help us find a very young mongoose to train as a pet.

"Memsahib, we do not like mongooses. They bring bad luck."

"Why is that?" I asked.

"They steal eggs, chase chickens, eat chicks. No good to village people. Villagers kill mongooses."

Maybe our promise to Steve hadn't been a good idea, but we had to try to honor it. So far, we had not met anyone who kept a pet mongoose. Could it be that Kipling's tale about his delightful pet in "Jungle Book" was just a tale? I talked to Steve and Donn about this possibility, but they both felt certain that such was not the case. I saw determination in their eyes.

One afternoon, I heard a light knock on the front door just before it squeaked open. A narrow-faced little creature stuck its head through the opening to peer over at me with iridescent chartreuse eyes.

"Well, hello, Little Critter. Are you a weasel in cat's clothing, or a cat in a weasel mask?" I asked.

"I'm Modhu, the mongoose," answered a tiny voice from behind the door, and in jumped my young son.

"She followed me out of the car, Mom. Can I keep her?"

He picked her up, and she cuddled in his arms like a kitten, for a moment. Then she climbed up onto his shoulder to wind her slender grizzly gray body over the back of his neck. Her long fluffy tail hung down to tickle his nose.

"*Modhu*, means "honey" in Bengali. She is a real honey, isn't she, Mom? Donn's friend gave her to him because his sister's cat had kittens. Mongooses like kittens, if you know what I mean. Her mother was a feral mongoose, killed by duck hunters, but one hunter took this baby home to raise as a pet. She is really well-trained already. Very smart, too."

Our boys had always had pets of one kind or another, from parakeets to guinea pigs, but this one was the most fun of all. Steve kept her on a string leash until she got acquainted with the household and its members. The servants skirted her at every opportunity, but she was quicker than a buttered eel.

Steve was teaching her the boundaries, which definitely excluded the kitchen. Smart though she was, she was still young and curious. She learned quickly that good things came from the kitchen.

Jahir Bux had become much more careful about all aspects of food preparation and refrigeration but he needed occasional reminders about keeping the eggs cold. He said they cooked better when they were warm, so he'd "forget" to put them away.

It didn't take Modhu long to train him. She escaped to the kitchen one morning when the eggs had been left out on the counter. She grabbed an egg, threw it against the white-washed wall, sucked out its contents and cleaned everything up with her rough tongue. She would have devoured every egg in sight had she not been caught. Steve found her just as the enraged cook was grabbing up the butcher knife.

A few days after the egg incident, our household was presented with a large green parrot, which, being a good luck omen, was meant to balance out Modhu's evil ways.

Modhu didn't view it that way. She saw this parrot as a challenge. Lucky's cage swung from the ceiling in the center of the screened verandah. This was of mighty interest to Modhu. She sat beneath it, hour after hour, her head moving in rhythm to the swinging of the cage. Sometimes she drooled.

Lucky showed only disdain for that loathsome mongoose. He hopped to the edge of the cage, looked down to take aim, and pushed piles of bird droppings and seed hulls on to Modhu's head.

It had to happen. One day we heard a wild squawking, as of a thousand mynah birds, coming from the verandah. Lucky was screeching curses from his safe perch on the window jam. Modhu was inside the cage, greedily chowing down bird seed. We settled Lucky's very ruffled feathers and then re-positioned the two animals. Modhu's boundaries were diminishing.

The affectionate little mongoose loved to be held, and we had agreed that she could sit on Steve's lap during meal times, as long as she did not show her head above the table. The night we had wild duck for dinner she forgot the boundary line. Perhaps it was the smell of the duck that brought out her feral ways. Just after Steve's duck was served, she reached up in a spasm of need, grabbed that bird off the plate, and carried it, her head held high, to the corner of the room.

"Modhu!" I yelled. "Drop that duck."

Modhu stopped. She fastened me with her glowing green eyes, and chomped defiantly on her forbidden fruit.

Sweet and tame though she was, she was still a feral animal. I knew better than to take her food away. I had to let her finish her stolen dinner, down to the last crunch of bone.

Then I picked her up, shook her a bit, and marched her out to the verandah.

"Naughty girl! Naughty girl!" I said, as I plunked her onto the floor.

Before I could get back through the door she had shot in and had marched over to the edge of the carpet in view of the diners. There she stopped to clean her whiskers. When I was sufficiently near, she glared into my face with daggers of crimson fury...as she made a big yellow puddle by the wall. "I am Modhu, the Riki Tiki Tavi of Bengal. Nobody messes with me."

CHAPTER 12 **THE GO-DOWN INCIDENT**

Chug...choke...burp...shudder, shudder. Silence. The death of the air conditioner in our bedroom woke me from an off-again, on-again night of sleep. The muggy monsoon air was steam-pressing my lungs. I struggled out from under the clammy sheet and staggered over to open the window in search of fresh air.

Whee-uw! The honey-bucket wagon must have passed recently. The stench made my eyes water. I slammed down the window and crawled back into bed, too drained to stay up. Anyway, it was too early.

I glanced over at Sahib, hoping that my rummaging around hadn't disturbed him. His pillow was wadded into a knot but no lump of body lay under the damp sheet. Poor guy, I guess he hadn't slept well either.

We had had a tiff the night before because I was enjoying the evening out with our new friends, and he wanted to go home before I was ready. We were both being stubborn, crossly making our points as we entered the side door of our house. We almost bumped into Jahir Bux, who was just coming out on his way back to his quarters. Embarrassed that our cook had heard us arguing we stopped bickering to wave him a cheery goodnight. Sahib put his arm around my shoulder as we walked into the house.

Now that the air conditioner had died, I could hear clattering and calling from the street, night sounds that melded into the new day's clamor. Above that, Sahib's baritone voice was speaking loudly to Jahir Bux.

I could hear china and silverware clanking, water splashing, a door slamming. 'What is going on?' I thought. 'Why is Sahib up so early? Has my clock stopped?'

Slowly the fog lifted. This was the day that Sahib was to go on a work visit to a remote station outside of Dacca—what we would call the "boondocks," in Bengal, called the *mofusils*. Back in The States, I would have been up getting his breakfast and seeing that all of his food and water needs for the trip were ready. I could get up now but Jahir Bux would probably tell me to get out of his kitchen, that he was taking care of Sahib. I might as well go back to sleep.

Instead, I watched the noisy gecko lizards create moving decorations on the ceiling. They scrambled about on hairy little suction cup feet, flicking up insects with greedy lasso tongues, and telegraphing their positions by calling "ge-cko." They delighted in waiting to answer "tik-tik" until the sleeper in the room dosed off. The apprehension always existed that those suction cups would fail at just the wrong time, like over the dining room table while we were eating soup...or like now as I, lying in bed, watched the one directly above me.

Negative thinking must have magnetic qualities. That scaly little reptile let go. He landed on my pillow and scrambled across my forehead with his scratchy toenails extended. Bra-a-ck!

I heard a bellow. For a moment I thought it was my echo. But no, it was Sahib yelling for me to come help him find the big yellow pads of paper he needed to take on his trip.

"If I don't get a move on, I'll miss the ferry!"

"I don't know where you put them," I yelled back. "Get some others from the go-down." (In America, it's a pantry).

My voice sounded as crabby as I felt. Lizard on my face, no sleep, putrid air...my excuses. But he must be feeling this way, too, besides having to go on a grueling trip during this monsoon misery. I didn't have to go anywhere. I didn't have to do anything, except to lie here and whine.

I jumped out of bed, pulling on my robe as I padded out to help Sahib. I could see his out-sized briefcase propped against the inner back verandah door. The breakfast table had been cleared, but odors of toast and egg lingered. I heard a toilet flush.

'Sahib's still here,' I thought. 'He's left the go-down door open, so he is expecting me to find those paper pads he needs. Otherwise he would have locked that door. It's our strict rule.'

My mind envisioned the location of the papers he needed, so without flipping on the light, I walked to the back of the narrow, cave-like pantry. SLAM! The door snapped shut. I was in a cavern of suffocating blackness.

"Hey!" I hollered, "I'm in here. Open the door."

I stopped calling for a second because I thought I heard the start of a car engine through the thin walls.

"Jahir Bux, stop Sahib. I am locked in the go-down."

Wheezy breathing from the other side of the door.

"Jahir Bux, has Sahib gone? Please answer me!"

"Hah-gee, Memsahib. Sahib gone now."

I didn't like being in this black confinement, but I wasn't going to panic. 'Just keep control, keep control.'

Calmly, I called, "Jahir Bux, please go to my bedroom dressing table and get the go-down key. It is in the small white box next to the mirror."

"I know, Memsahib."

'Yeh, I bet he does. Probably the whole household knows where we keep the key.'

The wheezy breathing outside the door continued. I did not hear footsteps padding away.

"Jahir Bux, did you understand me?" I tried to keep the frustration out of my voice.

"Hah-gee, Memsahib."

"Then GO! NOW!" I took deep, slow breaths. 'Stay calm. Stay calm.'

Jahir Bux went, but Jahir Bux did not return. I yelled. I hollered. I stomped my feet. I pounded on the door. I beat on the walls. Nothing.

I had not been an advocate of black, enclosed places ever since I was a snoopy five year old who got lost in a small cave. Like then, I didn't know how long I was going to be imprisoned, maybe all day if Jahir Bux didn't come back with the key.

I kicked and pounded on the door as I screeched, "Jahir Bux! Jahir Bux!"

All calm and logic were gone. I felt like I was being strangled.

Above my own din I heard a voice. I stopped yelling to listen. It sounded like Sahib. My heart stopped, shuddered like a worn-out engine, and started again.

The back screen door slammed. "Jahir Bux, where is Memsahib? I missed the ferry."

I heard Sahib's footsteps as he passed the go-down, so I started to pound and stomp and scream. "GET ME OUT OF HERE. I NEED TO KILL JAHIR BUX!"

Sweet sounds of rattling keys and the click of the lock. The door swung wide. Light and fresh air swept around me. I grabbed my husband and hung on, sobbing and pointing at Jahir Bux, who was standing at a safe distance behind Sahib.

"He knew I was locked in but he wouldn't let me out," I wailed.

Sahib turned to glare at Jahir Bux, and in a dark voice he asked, "Why did you not unlock the door for Memsahib?"

Jahir Bux's lower jaw stood open. He waggled his head back and forth, back and forth.

"But—but, Sahib," he stammered, "*YOU*, Master, *YOU* shut Memsahib in go-down. Only *YOU* must let Memsahib out!"

Poor Jahir Bux, small wonder he was confused. That's how it worked in his culture. I guess I couldn't kill him, after all.

But he'd better not push me!

CHAPTER 13   **MODHU, DECORATOR**

"It's movie night at US Information Service. Anyone want to go?" I asked during dinner.

It was a silly question because the alternative movie in Dacca would be a Bengali film, usually of poor quality, never in English, in an un-air-conditioned theater.

Not that our American film offerings were so great. They were always old ones most of us had seen before, and the film strip frequently broke during the most exciting scenes. We looked forward to them, though, as a change from our usual at-home card games and socializing.

This evening turned out to be no different. The film strip broke. The splicing wasn't successful. We returned home, dragging friends along for another night of chit-chat and listening to Cole Porter or the "Big Bands" on the tapes we shared with each other.

"Mom," Steve said the next morning, "My buddies and I are tired of swimming parties at the Dacca Club, or sitting around listening to your music when the movies fail. We want to have a party for all of our classmates. At home, like you do. I sorta told them we could have it here at our house."

Before I could catch my breath he hurried on. "Can I tell them that next Saturday night would be OK?"

What could I say? Our house was big enough for a lot of kids, and we did have that upstairs flat roof. Some of the boys had tapes made from the latest "pop music" albums like the Beatles. There would be plenty of room to dance.

On the day of the party, the boys decided it was necessary to decorate the house. They were soon festooning the living room, dining room, sitting room, hallways with red, green, orange, blue paper ribbons. Streamers crisscrossed window valances and center hanging lamps. Upstairs in the party room, they hung gaudy silver and gold paper cut-outs, like the local people used for wedding decorations.

Enter Modhu. She sat quietly, gaping at the decorating procedures for many moments. Her chartreuse eyes glinted as she cocked her head from side to side.

Suddenly she jumped at a streamer, throwing her whole body into action to bring it to the floor. She tore at it, growling softly, until it seemed sufficiently dead. Then she went after other streamers, wildly tearing them and throwing them about.

Steve yelled, "Stop, Modhu! No!" But the more he yelled, and the more the boys chased her, the more she liked it.

It was like watching a football game, with Modhu as the quarterback. She eluded them all, even jumping for more streamers as she darted about.

At last, many dead paper ribbons later, Steve grabbed her from behind, and hauled poor little mewing Modhu off to her nest in his desk drawer. There she stayed until the party was over.

"You can't let Modhu out until we have re-rolled what decorations remain," I told Steve. "You may want them for future parties, and any paper products are hard to find."

Eventually, Steve opened the door for his naughty little pet, who seemed more subdued then we had ever seen her. Perhaps she was just sleepy, but she sat very still, appearing to listen to our every scolding word. Later we saw her in the garden, stalking the neighbor's white cat—her favorite outdoor game.

We both felt that her moment of madness had passed. She would be a good little mongoose until we returned from the school function we had to attend.

Who knows? Was she feeling remorseful and wanted to make amends? Or did she just like the decorative effect?

For, when we returned in about two hours, we found a newly re-decorated house. Dear Modhu had gone to each of the three bathrooms to gather her decorating supplies. Toilet paper streamers festooned every piece of furniture, each window sill, the halls, the stairway and up to the party room—everywhere she could reach as long as the supply of toilet paper lasted.

Modhu, the mongoose extraordinaire, had paid her penance! It makes one wonder what she could have done with paints.

CHAPTER 14 **TO MARKET, TO MARKET**

Since the go-down fiasco, Jahir Bux was less mouthy and imperious. Perhaps his attitude had improved because I had tried to show more understanding. Anyway, I had made the decision to keep him on as cook because, from what the other memsahibs said, Jahir Bux was as good a cook as any of the local ones, and he was a star at specialty cooking.

On the strength of this higher comfort level between us, I said to Jahir Bux one early morning, "I would like to go with you to do the marketing today. Sahib wants me to see more of Dacca."

Sahib never knew how often his name was used to support my causes because its use always produced the desired effects.

"Hah-gee, Memsahib!"

I knew his enthusiasm was based on his getting a ride to market. On ordinary days he was expected to use his bicycle or a ricksha for shopping trips. The car and driver were for Sahib's job, and sometimes for Memsahib's use, not for the cook. So with Memsahib along, he could ride to market in style.

"Meat market day, Memsahib. William take us Old Dacca."

I had assumed that we would be going to the smaller, near-by New Market, but seeing Old Dacca and all the fascinating little shops for the first time would be much more fun.

William cleared his throat, frowned deeply and shook his head at Jahir Bux.

The cook turned his back on William. "Come, Memsahib." His hair flew into his face as he flipped his head to the side. "We go Old Dacca."

He jumped into the front seat of the vehicle, and looking straight ahead, he ordered, "Go, William. Go!"

William waggled his head and muttered, "Old Dacca market day no good for Memsahib."

I settled quickly into the back seat of the car, not having waited for the protocol of the driver to open my door. I was afraid he would find an excuse not to take us.

I took William's attitude lightly. This was a mere rooster fight. Let them go at it. I wanted to see the meat market, the many little shops, to feel the ancient history of the place.

The closer we got to the old part of Dacca, the narrower the roads became, and the more horn honking William did. The air space was filled with the raucous sounds of vehicles. The saying was that you could drive a car in Pakistan without brakes, as long as it had a horn. In this jam you couldn't go fast enough for brakes, but the car's 'voice' was a must! Almost every mode of transportation was on that road: trucks, autos, buses, bicycle rickshas, bullock carts, closed horse-drawn carriages, all of them honking, beeping, dinging or blowing whistles...no two melodies the same.

Vendors pitched their wares loudly, hawking nose-tickling spices or red clay pots. Grubby brown urchins, dragging tiny naked tots, darted between vehicles, or followed bony cows to catch the hot manure. A hollow-eyed beggar shoved his battered tin bowl through the window nearest to me. He sing-songed a whine, begging for alms.

One bare-chested man, carrying a baby goat around his neck like a scarf, bumped into a bus in front of us in his haste to get to the big market. The kid bawled its complaint. The man cursed the bus driver for being in his way.

What a beehive! So much activity was taking place that I could hardly absorb all the sights and sounds. The smells I would have been happy to eliminate: body sweat, open sewer drains, bullock droppings, to name a few.

Like a beehive, everyone was intent on his plan of action for that day. No lollygaggers here! This was like watching a movie. It was enthralling, and I was so glad I had ignored William.

But that was before I got out of the car.

The turtle-paced traffic became a clogged drain. William inched the car to the side of the road and stopped.

He glowered at Jahir Bux, "Take Memsahib now. You walk to market from here."

"Memsahib!" He frowned at me. "You must be careful. Stay close behind Jahir Bux. Too many people today. Do not lose him!"

I paid no attention to the black cloud warning in William's voice. The energy of this mass of humanity was drawing me like a bee to sweet red clover. I hopped out of the back seat to catch up with Jahir Bux, who was already elbowing a trail for me. I had to hurry, watching that nobody could jam into the momentary empty space between the jabs.

My pink cotton dress was soon clinging to my body with sweat. I was joining the ranks of the rank. The enchantment was gone.

All I could see were bodies pushing each other to get ahead or around, or like Jahir Bux was doing, through.

I was sure Jahir Bux was just ahead of me. That was his broad back in the loose white shirt. But when he turned his head sideways I saw a hawk nose, not Jahir Bux's plump round one. Almost every person in this crowd was wearing a loose white shirt. How long had I been following the wrong man? I panicked. My heart went crazy. I gasped for breath. Why hadn't I listened to William? This was not a crowd to be lost in.

I bolted forward as hard as I could, peering, searching ahead for a sight of Jahir Bux, not daring to call out his name. What if many men in East Bengal had that name? I might be surrounded with Jahir Buxes. What a thought!

Suddenly I was shoved from behind. My right foot struck a soft object on the ground, causing me to trip. But I was held upright by this bulk of human traffic, rushing onward like a river in spate. Where would I end up? This was big trouble!

A strong hand grabbed my arm from behind, forcing me to push through the mass of bodies ahead of me. Ice numbed my muscles. My heart did a Highland fling.

"Go, Memsahib, go! Push your way through. Hurry!" William's harsh whisper was in my ear.

I could not get a full breath.

"William, please let me stop," I whimpered. "I can't breathe."

"Hahgee, Memsahib, just a little way ahead people will turn off to market. Then we stop to rest." William's husky voice calmed me. My breathing returned.

Our progress was still a rapid forward push, shove and elbow but the movement gradually slowed.

My trembling legs were starting to sag by the time William whispered, "Here!" He guided me into a hut-size, upright wood shipping crate set into a recess at the side of the road.

It was probably someone's shelter, but no one was in it except for a huge black rat that scurried over my foot on its rush to escape. Too short of breath to scream, I just leaned against the wooden side and closed my eyes.

"William, what's happening? Why did you grab my arm and push me ahead so fast? Was someone bad following us? Where's Jahir Bux? What's going on?" I couldn't seem to shut up.

"This is a poor country, Memsahib. When a person who has no money is dying, his family lays him on a walkway for people to give alms for his burial. You are a rich American memsahib. You kicked a dying man. You did not leave alms. Someone noticed. He grabbed at you, but I saw. If he had been lucky, he would have caused you great trouble, demanding many rupees. If you could not pay, everyone in the crowd would have yelled at you and pulled at your clothes and your hair. They would have killed you if you did not please them, Memsahib. I am sorry, but it is our way. Now you understand."

I slumped to the floor of the packing crate, my knees like shifting sand. I was weak with shock. To think I had kicked a dying person, and hadn't even known it!

"I'm so sorry, William! I didn't know..." Through the lump in my throat, I managed to choke out, "And thank you for protecting me. You saved my life."

William ducked his head. "My duty, Memsahib. We cannot rest for long. You are not yet out of danger. Some people may still be hunting for you. I know a safer, but longer way to take."

He went over to a dark corner of the crate and picked up a filthy shawl, which he shook, causing dust, rat droppings and huge brown cockroaches to fly in every direction.

"Please to stand, Memsahib."

Obediently I stood on legs that wobbled like a marionette's. He handed me that nasty rag, and said, "You must cover your red hair and white face with this dupatta. Perhaps you will not be so much noticed."

Never Cheat A Holy Man

I pulled the awful thing over my hair and close around my face, holding it to keep it from sliding off. The putrid smell made me gag, but I held it in place as we ducked out of the wooden enclosure. William went ahead of me now, which was seemly, since it was the custom for the woman to walk behind the man. The crowd had thinned enough so that we could go more slowly.

I moved my feet with great caution, fearful of kicking another dying person.

William had said this would be a long route back to the car. It felt to me as though we were walking the circumference of planet Earth at the equator. The sun was blistering. The stinking rag on my head was nauseating me. My throat stuck together with dryness.

William happened to glance back just as I was starting to remove the dupatta for a snatch of fresh air. He shook his head vigorously.

"No, no, Memsahib. Do not take off dupatta until we are in the car. Almost there."

Vomit rose up to burn in my throat, but I swallowed it down. I owed so much to William that I wasn't about to complain. If he said it wasn't safe yet, I'd believe him. The shawl stayed on.

"What do you think happened to Jahir Bux?" I asked, suddenly remembering how I had gotten into this mess.

"Not to worry about that scoundrel. He is probably home by now." William's mouth curled downward in disdain. "I told him not wise to take Memsahib today. Market day is crazy day, but Jahir Bux selfish man. Thinks only to get ride. Bah!"

In a few more minutes we were back at the car. Jahir Bux was leaning casually against it, chatting with a friend. He held up a dripping bundle.

"Meat, Memsahib. You missed meat market. William make mistake. He push you beyond the turn." He sneered at William.

If looks could kill, Jahir Bux, *pukka cook and major-domo* would have been lying dead at the feet of driver William, who squeezed his lips until there were none showing. We drove home in complete silence. That didn't include the horn, of course. It got the work-out of its life.

So much for my staying out of the way to observe. The fault was mine that cook and driver were now at odds. William had been protecting me. It was his job. He had warned Jahir Bux, who willfully did not listen. I had also heard the warning, but had not wished to heed. It was easy to be mad at Jahir Bux about this but I knew the fault wasn't all his.

I did wonder if Jahir Bux was ensuring his job in our household by letting me learn the inconveniences of the role he played, and the dangers I could encounter should I decide to do the cooking myself, like some of the memsahibs were doing. After the experience I had today at the market, he could be safe from that worry...although I'll never tell him so.

CHAPTER 15 **NO EXCUSES SHORT OF PLAGUE OR RABIES**

The good will I had begun to feel toward Jahir Bux had evaporated after the market incident. As much as I hated to upset the otherwise well-oiled machinery of the household, the idea of replacing Jahir Bux was beginning to appeal to me again.

I talked to the other family members about sacking him because of his bad attitude toward me, but they protested.

"Any cook you hire will be the same," they whined. "Jahir Bux finally knows how to cook the foods we like. We haven't gotten sick yet because he keeps things clean. And besides, you have to admit he's good at handling parties. Just stay out of his way."

Easy for them to say. How did they think he learned to fix those foods? Who did they think was really responsible for keeping them healthy? But they were right about his ability to work under the pressure of entertaining. He was stellar at those times.

Yes, they were right. I was letting him get under my skin. And to be practical, I would not have time to train a new cook properly because I had recently accepted a temporary job as the American Consulate nurse. I would have to stand away and give him room to operate on his own. Scary!

Every morning before I went to work I laid out supplies from the go-down, to give him ideas for things he might build meals around. Using what he needed, he could plan menus from those foods, plus daily market produce. Jahir Bux was pleased with this arrangement because he now had control. He swaggered more than ever but was less overbearing with me. He got along fairly well with the other servants, except, of course, for the dhobi, and lately, the young kitchen helper.

Isham came to Sahib one day, red-faced and tearful. "Jahir Bux cook, mean man. I quit!"

Jahir Bux flipped the lad off with, "Lazy, stupid boy. Better he go."

He didn't ask to hire another helper, which surprised me because he would now have to do the menial kitchen tasks so beneath his lofty position of *pukka cook and major-domo*.

One morning I returned to the house unexpectedly to find Jahir Bux snoring in the hammock on the back verandah. I slammed the screen door, but the sleeping prince snoozed on.

Water was running in the nearby kitchen so I hurried in to investigate. Chaos! The garden boy was squatting barefoot inside the large cement floor-sink. He was splashing our breakfast dishes under the cold water to wash them. As I watched, he took a greasy rag from around his neck to dry the dishes. On the cement counter were toast bits afloat in melted water buffalo butter. A gorge of blue bottle flies serenaded them. A basketful of eggs gleamed ecru in the blazing sun.

"Jahir Bux!" I screeched. "Come into this kitchen *NOW*."

Jahir Bux staggered through the door, rubbing blurry, half-opened eyes.

"What is the meaning of this? You know the rules." My voice crackled with fury.

"Oh, Memsahib," he moaned, rubbing his forehead and rocking his body. "I suffer. suffer! Very hurt head today."

Perhaps he was sick today, but "he suffered, he suffered" all too frequently, like when it was time to do mundane chores, or when he needed an excuse for having returned late from his vacation. Kobad had taken up the slack in the past. But Kobad was off on leave this week. To my mind, Jahir Bux's suffering was open to question.

"All right, Jahir Bux," I said in my sternest memsahib voice, "Dismiss the mali to his garden duties, and NEVER bring him into this kitchen again. If you are so sick that you have been willing to break all the rules that keep this family well, go take a headache pill and lie down in your quarters. I will clean up this mess and prepare dinner. Sahib will see you later."

Jahir Bux had been looking down at his feet until I mentioned Sahib. Then his head jerked up. He stammered, "Head better now, Memsahib. You go your job. I clean. I cook."

"Jahir Bux, you know the rules: "Number One," I said, sticking out my right thumb, "No garden workers are to come into this kitchen. The soil they bring in carries germs which can make this family very sick.

"Number Two," I stabbed toward him with my pointing finger. "All dishes must be washed and rinsed in boiling water; then air-dried only.

"Number Three," my middle finger jabbed almost into his chin. "All water must be boiled for at least twenty minutes.

"Number Four, "All vegetables must be cleaned thoroughly, rinsed well in iodine water, then cooked. Serve nothing raw. Meats must be rinsed with iodine water before being well cooked."

I picked up the basket of eggs and swung them in front of him. "*NEVER, NEVER LEAVE EGGS OUT.*"

Jahir Bux hung his head as I ticked off the rules. "I know, Memsahib," he mumbled. "You go now."

It was as close to contrition as I had seen from him.

A week passed without incident, and another week. I checked the kitchen each morning and evening, and always found them sparklingly clean. Jahir Bux knew that his job hung by a wisp of rice straw. I began to feel optimistic.

One evening in my third week, I came home exhausted after a frustrating day of giving immunizations to villagers. Some of them thought that if one shot was good, a second would be better, so they kept getting back into line. Others, afraid of the needle, would convince a relative to take the shot for them. This confusion took a lot of sorting out. We worked through lunch. By the time I got home I felt capable of eating an elephant, a toad and two goldfish.

Right behind me came Sahib, equally drained and hungry after another two-day trip to the mofusils. Soon, young Sahib bounced through the door in his "What's to eat?" teen-age mode.

The house was quiet. No activity in the kitchen. The supplies I had left out for Jahir Bux were still where I had placed them. There were no signs of dinner preparations. We looked and called for Jahir Bux, but we couldn't find him anywhere around the premises. None of the servants, not even the chowkidar had seen him all day.

I opened a can of beans and some little tinned sausages to heat up for a quick supper. The stove would not light. No kerosene! This was not one of Jahir Bux's finer days! By the time we had sat down to eat our miserable cold dinner, I had run out of superlatively mean words to say about Jahir Bux. For once, the sahibs were with me. We were a united front against our cook, the "sufferer." No excuse short of the plague or rabies was going to save his job.

About midnight, a heavy pounding on my bedroom door brought me upright out of a deep sleep.

Jahir Bux was sobbing and calling, "Doctah Memsahib, save me. I die! I die!"

"Great performance," I muttered to my groggy husband. "At least he isn't saying he's suffering. Now he just outright dies! This had better be good."

I yanked yesterday's smelly top over my head, wiggled into a wrinkled skirt, and slid into sloppy rubber sandals. So much for the "doctah's" uniform.

Out on the verandah, Jahir Bux was holding his right arm as he paced the floor. When he saw me he began to gabble hysterically. He shoved his arm close to my face, sobbing, "See, Memsahib, see!"

In the bright light of the living room lamp, I could see a puncture bite just above his wrist.

"Doctah Memsahib, crazy dog run out of bushes, attack me. Then it run down road and jump into ricksha. Someone screaming. Dog bite ricksha man, too. It is rabies dog, I know!"

Jahir Bux began to rock his body and wail. "I don't want to die like that. Please to save me, Memsahib. Please to save me!"

The wound was clearly an animal bite, and by his description of the incident it probably was a rabid animal. Sick and starving pariah dogs roamed the streets of Dacca, grubbing into the garbage dumps to keep alive. Very few animals were immunized in Pakistan.

The victim of rabies without immediate treatment was doomed to an agonizing death. In the villages, a rabies victim was isolated in a separate hut, food and water pushed through the door, and the patient left alone. Fear of contracting the disease caused terror in any village. Jahir Bux had seen this. He knew I was not a doctor, but a nurse in a position to get the vaccine that could save his life.

I had been told that the local rabies vaccine was always in short supply, and not very reliable when it was available. Many villagers did not even know that a rabies vaccine existed. They relied on their village hakim, medicine man, for treatment of their illnesses. He had many ancient and useful concoctions, but nothing to cure rabies. Thank goodness, Jahir Bux had come to us for help.

"You are going to be all right, Jahir Bux. We will start you on the anti-rabies vaccine right away," I soothed him, as I cleansed the wound.

Meanwhile, my husband and sons went out to search for the rabid dog. They didn't find the animal, but a few blocks down the street they found an empty, tipped-over ricksha. No one was around, which was unusual, even for the middle of the night. Word of rabies strikes deeply into the hearts of those who have seen cases of the disease. The police would have to be notified right away, in case they had not already been informed.

Every morning for the next fourteen days, Jahir Bux lay calmly on Young Sahib's bed, baring his fat, brown belly to "Doctah Memsahib's" needle. He was truly brave, hardly flinching as the stinging vaccine pierced his skin. After each injection he said,"*Donabad*, Memsahib. Thank you!" and never again did he say, "I suffer, I suffer."

The American vaccine did its work, and from then on, so did Jahir Bux!

CHAPTER 16 **MODHU TO THE RESCUE**

When we had first come to Dacca, Habib had said that the Foundation would pay for new curtaining if we wanted to use local fabric. I looked for several weeks in many of the "sari" shops before I found just the right color –a filmy green-blue that suggested the coolness of a misty sea.

Modhu quietly watched the curtain-hanging from her favorite settee cushion. Lately she had settled down so well that I forgot about her propensity for getting into mischief.

But with a sudden leap, she bounded onto the nearest curtain, twisting and bouncing. Then she climbed to the top of it and jumped to the next one, and the next. She was behaving like a baby Tarzan, and she was going to ruin my new curtains.

"Get out of there, you bad girl!" I yelled, as I grabbed her off the shredding fabric. "These are not trees for you to climb on." I carried her out to her favorite Causarina tree. "Climb here."

Apparently she understood, because she stopped climbing the curtains.

Early one very steamy morning, a Pakistani lady came to our compound gate. "Chowkidar, you will go tell your memsahib that I wish to see her. Do not keep me waiting."

"Ha gee, Begum. I will announce." He shuffled off to tell the butler's helper, leaving the woman outside the gate.

The butler's helper stopped for tea before he remembered to inform the cook, who took his time to tell Kobad, who thought I was asleep, and was slow to knock on my bedroom door.

"Memsahib, a Pakistani lady is outside gate," he called.

"Thank you, Kobad. Please go invite the poor woman inside. It must be hot out there."

I peeked out of my dressing room window to see a very plump woman huffing up the driveway. She was shaking her finger and scolding at Kobad as she swirled her volume of green-blue sari up the verandah steps.

"Please come inside where it is cool," I called to her. "Kobad will get you nimbu pani. I will be with you in a minute."

Suddenly I heard a banshee scream coming from the living room. I ran in to find the begum jumping around and beating at her sari skirt like she was on fire.

"Modhu!" I yelled. "Get out of there NOW!"

Modhu gave a squeak and tumbled onto the floor at the woman's feet. Her face was fire-engine red, and her eyes had begun to bulge. Before I could even apologize, she had flown out the door like a sheet in a hurricane.

I never found out why she had come, and never saw her again. But I knew why she had run off in such a hurry. She had been "attacked" by a mongoose, which, to a Bengali is the worst possible bad luck. Her bad luck really was that her sari and my curtains were made of the same fabric, and Modhu could not discriminate.

I was furious with that little animal. She hadn't meant to attack the lady, I knew. Still, just because her Causarina tree walked into the house, she didn't get an automatic license to climb. By the time I had finished upbraiding her and shoving her out the door, Modhu knew without any doubt that she had done something very wrong. I had no intention of letting her back in the house for a long time. Steve sneaked her in later on, but she kept well out of my sight.

The pre-monsoon season of April and early May is miserably humid, the most uncomfortable weather of the year. One could shower hourly, yet feel itchy and sticky five minutes later.

I was still mentally threatening Modhu as I prepared for one of my frequent showers. Clothes off, towel handy, shower tap turned on. I stepped into the shower stall and watched the cool water run off my fingertips—directly onto the fanned and swaying head of a COBRA.

I held my breath and slowly backed out of the stall, the shower curtain swinging behind me.

"Help! Cobra in my shower. Modhu, come!" My scream was loud enough to intimidate even a snake. It didn't budge this one.

But Modhu arrived as swiftly as only a mongoose can do. Right behind her came Kobad and Jahir Bux.

Modhu whisked into the bathroom, but the men covered their eyes and did a swirling about-face.

'Sissies,' I thought. 'A lot of help they are. Look how brave Modhu is.'

That's when I caught a glimpse of myself in the mirror. In my excitement at seeing the snake I had forgotten that I was nude.

Jahir Bux never looked directly at me again, and Kobad was too embarrassed to come back into the house for two days.

In the meantime, Modhu went after that cobra with the enthusiasm of a cowboy trying to win a gold buckle at a bull riding event. She was wonderfully agile as she kept that snake's fangs away from herself. Her teeth clenched onto the back of its neck, swinging and shaking until it was dead. Then she proudly pushed it back down the open drain from which it had crawled.

At last I understood that all that climbing and jumping and racing about, for which I had scolded and finally banned her, was training for her greatest performance—killing a cobra to rescue her memsahib.

CHAPTER 17 **THE SNAKE AND THE DRAGON LADY**

Hoorah! The end of October. The last of the monsoon swelters and sogs. The cooling restless breezes of winter stirred, and so did I.

"Hey, Chota Sahib," I teased, "Let's go look for an adventure. How about a picnic in the country?"

No school that day, Sahib was out of town, the vehicle was mine to use. I wasn't supposed to take the car without a driver because the Foundation considered memsahibs unsafe without an escort. But William, my usual escort-driver, was away on holiday. Steve and I could escort each other today, and take advantage of this rare opportunity to do something fun alone together.

I hurried to the go-down and took out the only can of ham. A ham sandwich would taste so good. Jahir Bux had gone to his village for a holiday so I could use MY kitchen to open the ham. I would have to clean up thoroughly so he would never know that such unclean food as pig meat had contaminated HIS kitchen. The Muslim servants were never asked to handle pork foods but I could do it myself today, disposing of the metal container through Joseph, who was Christian.

This canned ham was the only one of the six we had ordered that had reached us without nails stabbed into it. If a particularly zealous Muslim customs official had been on duty the day our order arrived from Denmark, we could not be sure how much of it we'd get, or what its condition would be. Especially pig products, which were forbidden foods to faithful Muslims.

After we had checked through the shipment of the last order, I had said to Jahir Bux, "I understand that there is a Muslim taboo against pork, which explains why someone destroyed most of our cans of ham, but why did they spoil the canned turkey?"

He shook his head, looking at me with sad dark eyes, as though there was no hope for me.

"Mohammed had chin whiskers. Turkeys have chin whiskers. To eat such a creature would be an insult to the sacred name of Mohammed."

"I see," I said, "but what about the special candy treats I had ordered for Chota Sahib's birthday? You can't tell me that Islam has a taboo against candy. It is sold on the streets all the time. My order was just plain stolen."

"Oh, no, Memsahib! Customs officer is Gov'ment man. Not allowed to steal. He only take his bakshish." (The interpretation of bakshish is very loose—a tip or a bribe, or in this case, theft).

Steve and I soaked up the clean green of the countryside as we drove over the roads, still sticky with red mud from the last of the monsoon drips. I never tired of watching the naked youngsters race each other on the narrow paddy levees. Their sari-clad mothers often swayed along behind, balancing two or three brown clay pots on their heads. These rural Bengalis restored my sense of serenity. I could feel their contentment, the rhythm in their lives. Out here the breeze carried a sweet perfume—with just a touch of bullock droppings to define its rural nature.

Steve broke my reverie with, "Hey, Mom. Here's a great picnic spot."

He was pointing to a huge banyan tree. Its many aerial roots stabbed the ground, giving it several smaller trunks. Its branches looked like long-stretching arms, dressed in a garment of shiny leaves. I got out of the car for a closer look. Steve grabbed the water jug and the metal tiffin container and hurried over to examine our picnic location.

"Nice shade," I said. "Let's eat right here. We can lean against the tree trunk."

"Mom, we can't do that! We'll have to climb the tree. Don't you know there are snakes here? Kobad warns me all the time."

I wasn't prepared for climbing trees, having worn a western-style dress with a short skirt, and a pair of flip-floppy shoes. But neither was I prepared to share my precious ham sandwich, or myself, with a snake. Flip-flops don't make great climbing shoes, especially on the smooth bark of a banyan, but with two steps up and one slide back, I followed my monkey-climber son up to the wide branch that made a perfect bench.

We opened our three-tiered lunch bucket, our mouths watering for those sandwiches.

"Tee hee hee." Giggling from below. Where had they come from, this bunch of semi-naked little boys who had appeared out of the vapor? They waved to us, and some of the tinier ones reached their arms up, waggling their fingers in that universal sign of "gimme."

There were too many kids for two sandwiches, and if these were Muslim children we couldn't give them ham. We removed the ham for ourselves and tossed pieces of bread down to them. That caused a brief tussle, which occupied their time while we savored our meat. I had thrown in a couple of finger-length lemon bananas, so much better than the bananas we got in the States. Those, we ate without guilt, knowing that bananas were daily fare to these youngsters. But we left our dessert in the lunch box, because two small cookies would only be enough for one small mouth. We didn't want to start a major food riot. We gulped big drafts of water, and called it lunch.

The kids were getting noisy, jumping and yelling, "Baba, ao! Ao, Baba!"

Sometimes Kobad referred to Steve affectionately as "Baba," so I figured the boys just wanted this new kid to come play. One big slide, and Steve was down the tree trunk. I'd thought to stay until after the kids had moved off a bit. But they kept shouting and calling. I knew there was a reason to move when I heard Steve's voice urgently yelling, "Mom! Get down!"

I reached out to brace myself, holding onto one of the aerial branches as I started the descent.

The branch began to writhe. Steve screamed, "Snake! Python!"

The plunge to the ground was easier than the landing, which broke my sandal and twisted my ankle. But that didn't stop my running like I was sprinting for first place in an Olympic race.

The children waited for me as we headed for a nearby village. When we reached its boundary of bamboo hedges, I hesitated. I was not there by adult invitation. Maybe the villagers would resent my intrusion.

But the kids wanted to show off their new friends, pulling us into the midst of the village women. They all jabbered at once as they pointed to the big tree, mimicking how Memsahib was up in the tree, holding onto the snake, and had flown out of the tree just like a bird!

The older women smiled, but they stayed back, eyeing me closely. The young ones laughed and mimicked the boys. Some of the girls sidled closer to examine my short auburn hair, and to pinch at the freckles on my face. They giggled and whispered to each other.

Even the toddlers were curious. Their grimy baby fingers rubbed up and down my legs. One kid took a sharp baby-toothed nibble. I yelped. He wailed. After that, no other babies tried to taste me.

The older women, encouraged by their sons' friendliness toward the foreign boy, pulled "Baba" into their group for further examination. I watched nervously as they rubbed strands of his light blond hair through their dark fingers, and leaned in to stare at his purple-blue eyes. I admired his quiet, smiling manner while the ladies looked him over to make certain that his strangeness would not rub off on their kids. Soon the little boys, bored with waiting, dragged him away to show him their village.

After that, I relaxed, playfully checking out my young audience. I fingered the long thick braid of a doe-eyed girl with a red Hindu dot on her forehead, and ruffled the curly hair of a three year old whose plump belly hung over a fragment of skirt. The eyes of every small child and baby were decorated with black eyeliner, an antimony mixture, meant to prevent eye disease. It made their beautiful dark eyes look enormous.

I picked up one of the crawling babies, who howled, and pushed to get away. Suddenly the women and girls pulled back and grew silent. I sucked in my breath, certain I had offended them. I set the baby down fast, and looked contrite.

But they were not noticing me at all; rather, they were looking at a hut which was toward the center of the village and larger than the other huts. A hunched old woman hobbled out from its narrow doorway. She leaned forward to brand me with her fire-eating eyes. Her face was so twisted into a grimace that her upper lip touched her long nose. A Dragon Lady, I thought!

This woman, right here, was the reason I had been reluctant to enter the village uninvited. By the reaction of the other women, she was the ruling force of this extended family—the mother-in-law. If she did not want me in her village, she could set the others against me.

The snake hadn't scared me nearly as much as this woman did. Not having a tree to jump out of, or behind, I stood, rooted in place.

Dragon Lady kept her eyes glued on me as she shuffled in my direction, ignoring the red mud spattering her ankles and up onto her dingy white sari.

I forced a smile, putting my shaking hands together in the Hindu namaste greeting and slight bow of respect.

She grunted. She did not greet. She moved closer and closer, her eyes gliding up and down my body, feet to head, head to feet.

Finally she spoke to me, but in Bengali. I didn't understand, but the others knew what she had asked because they gasped and rolled their eyes as they moved nearer.

Now she was very close to me. Mentally I prepared for an attack. She planted herself in front of me, her head angled in question.

Then, in one flashing movement of her talon-like fingers, she lifted my short skirt, and bent to look underneath. Shocked, I grabbed at her sari skirt, which, being long, didn't pull up very far.

It occurred to me then, that this was ridiculous: Two women from different worlds, each trying to see what the other wore under her skirt. I looked full into the eyes of this formidable woman—and laughed.

She tipped her head to the other side, scowled. Then, she too, burst out in a harsh cackle. The other village women howled with laughter, dancing around and clapping their hands.

Dragon Lady never did find out what I was wearing under my skirt, nor do I know what was under her sari.

But I do know that the tea she served was delicious.

CHAPTER 18 ARE YOU SLEEPING, SISTER MARIE, SISTER MARIE?

"I am Sister Marie, and I'm from da Bronx, New Yawk." The nun's exuberant voice halted the chatter of the ladies at the American Consulate Welcome Tea.

I turned to see a woman the size of a tackle for the New York Giants, sweeping from table to table. Her white nun's garb added flare to the flamboyant way she greeted everyone. She stopped to ask where various ladies had come from, or how long they had been in Dacca. She responded with "oh's" and "ah's," bits of profanity thrown in. Each time she let such a word slip out, she slapped her hand over her mouth. "Still learning," she'd say.

Some of the more proper ladies, whose husbands were with important government missions, looked askance and whispered behind their white gloved hands. But I liked her immediately. She was so open, so unpretentious.

Sister Marie had just come to East Pakistan to work as a nurse at the Leprosarium, a Catholic-run community about forty miles from Dacca.

"I had begged and begged for Mother Superior to send me to work among the lepers. I felt it was my calling. Of course I had the Hawaii colony in mind." She laughed and rolled her eyes.

"But the Good Lord saw it otherwise, and so I have landed in the damnedest (mouth slap), strangest country I know nothing about. Oh, well, I shall bull my way through."

Her vigorous laugh rattled the windows as she added, "I hope you will all come to visit me, though perhaps not all at one time."

Several weeks had passed when a large box arrived at the American Consulate addressed to Sister Marie c/o the East Pakistan Leprosarium. I offered to take the package to the nun since I had not yet visited this Leprosarium, nor any other. Leprosy, or its new name of Hansen's Disease, was one of the many tropical diseases I was eager to learn about.

She sent a quick response to my note about the trip. I had asked what special tidbits I could bring along for her.

Dear Mrs. Joy,

I'll be so happy to see a familiar English-speaking person. You will be surprised to know that I am learning not to be profane. The patients are picking up on my English much too fast! Anything at all you bring will be wonderful. Anything, that is, except rice. We have rice three times a day, for which I must be duly thankful. This is very difficult for me because I detest rice...always have. God knows that, too. He is surely testing me.

'Til soon, Yours, in His Blessed Love,
Sister Marie.

The village compound was in a wide clearing of deep jungle. It included a dispensary, a chapel, and several low airy buildings for the patients and staff. It was as clean as any Bengali village could possibly be during the non-stop rains of the monsoon season.

Sister Marie greeted me boisterously, dragging me to her quarters to open her new box of goodies. She almost choked me to death with hugs when she saw the cans of beer.

"Oh, Mrs. Joy! Real American beer. That kerosene-tasting local hooch is so bad, I was afraid I'd have to swear off beer, too. What would my friends in the Bronx say!"

The large box that had come from the States was hauled into the dispensary, where Sister rang a big brass bell. Patients, all men and boys, came from the various huts and buildings in the compound. Most were adults, some with stumped limbs or missing fingers or toes. Others were blind, being led by sighted patients. Still others had damaged facial features of bumps, scars and openly eroded areas. I was as friendly in my greeting as possible, but inside I felt shocked; hoped it didn't show.

But Sister Marie could tell, and in her ebullient way, she rescued me. "We have prepared a special program just for you, Mrs. Joy." She turned to the patients, beating her foot for rhythm.

"Ek, do, tin," (one, two, three). And off they went. Those who could dance began the steps. Those who could clap pounded their hands together. All who could, began to sing. It was a simple folk song about fishing, about the beauty of their land and their loveliest maidens.

A shy little boy with sparkling black eyes and a bandaged foot pulled me into the group. We all laughed at the awkward way I tried to do their dance steps. It was a workout!

"Sister," I said, after we had rested a bit, "I'd like to teach them a round, with your help."

She separated the patients into three groups, explaining in Bengali what we were going to do.

"It goes like this," and I started to sing, "Are you sleeping, are you sleeping, Sister Marie, Sister Marie?" to the tune of 'Frere Jacque.' They were quick to pick up the tune, even gabbling through the English. They shouted out the "SISTER MARIE" part, clapping and stomping at the "Dong! Ding! Dee!"

When the song ended, Sister jumped up from her chair, slapping her thighs. "Now, time for the Great Box Opening!" she shouted.

Everyone was counting on what was to be in that box. A letter from Sister Marie's home diocese had foretold the imminent arrival of the desperately needed new bandages and other medical supplies.

The patients gathered close, prepared to "Achha!" (Yeah!), as Sister ripped open the box. A barely audible curse slid from between her compressed lips as she unfurled a long snake-like roll of knitted wool "bandage." She pulled out roll after roll of those hot, heavy items, things impossible to use in the humid tropical heat of East Pakistan.

Silently the patients began to leave, heads down, shoulders slumped.

Nothing else was in that box.

"Wait, Everyone!" boomed Sister Marie. "It is clear that we can't use these like they are now but we must remember that the ladies of our church in America spent many hours knitting them for us. They thought it would be as cold here as it is in New Yawk in winter, and wanted us to be warm." Snorts and groans from the patients. "They have been praying for us in our times of need. Now we must find a way to put these to our good use so that we can be grateful for their kind deeds. Gather round and let's think of a plan."

"Sister," I broke in, not wanting to have to interrupt their conference later on. "It's a long drive back to Dacca, so I must leave now. Thank you, Everyone."

My sparkly-eyed little friend grabbed my hand and thumped along with Sister Marie and me to the car. "Sista Marie, Sista Marie. Dong, Ding, Dee! Dong, Ding, Dee!" he sang in lusty little-kid voice as he waved goodbye.

Another two months passed before I saw Sister Marie again. She limped into the American Consulate nursing office with a rain-cloud expression on her face and a tremble in her much more subdued voice. She pulled up the skirt of her habit to show me an open tear on the meaty calf of her right leg.

"Last night a crazed wild dog raced out of the jungle and attacked me. If the night chowkidar had not shot him, that animal would have killed me." Her voice broke into little sobs. "As it is, I'll die the slow way—of rabies."

She laid her head on the examination table, and bawled. The fear, the pain, the exhaustion of the journey into Dacca had shattered her.

She continued to shiver and cry as I examined the extent of the wound. Finally, through jerks and sniffles, she was able to talk.

"I always hated being big and fat. My secret prayer was that when it was my turn to leave this Earth I would get a fading-away disease that would turn me pale and beautiful and, at last, delicately thin." She began to wail, "But, no! Instead I must drool and bubble, have agonizing seizures, to end up dying alone, everyone afraid to be near me. And I'm still going to be FAT!" Her whole body shook as she rocked back and forth, her hands tight around her rosary.

"Sister!" I shook her shoulder and leaned into her face, "We have American vaccine here. The treatments can be started right away, without waiting for the results of the lab report from the dog. You will need an injection every day for fourteen days, and you know that they sting like bee bites, but they are life savers! No drools and bubbles for you."

She grabbed me up in an elephantine hug. "Oh, Mrs. Joy, thank you!" she cried.

After her series of treatments had been completed, her leg wound healing well, and no sign of rabies, Sister Marie hurried back to her village.

"Next time I see you," she had said between smothering farewell hugs, "I will show you the magic my dear ones at the Leprosarium are performing."

The ladies of the Women's Club had been advertising their "Tea and Everything" charity sale for several weeks. We all donated new and used items from our pantries and closets. We baked goods to sell with the tea, just like back home in the States.

The day before the Big Day, I got a note from Sister Marie.

Please reserve a table for me. I am bringing our exciting new products for everyone to admire, and, of course to buy. See you tomorrow.

Hugs, hugs, Sister Marie

The meeting room was barely set up when a bevy of begums and memsahibs crowded through the door. The more westernized Pakistani women, the begums, usually had more rupees to spend than articles they wanted to buy, other than beautiful sari silks and gold filigreed jewelry. They did not want our outer garments other than casual button-up sweaters for cool evenings, but they hankered after dainty underwear. My neighbor once told me laughingly that she'd sell her first born daughter (not son, of course) for almost any major American appliance. By the way she went after the kitchen wares and appliances table at the sale, one could almost believe her. It was swept clean in the first ten minutes, amid much squabbling and hair pulling.

"Ladies! Ladies!" boomed a voice familiar to my ears. In bustled Sister Marie, her arms full of colorful items. "Gather round while I set up my table so that you may choose which of these lovely rugs and placemats, coasters and wall hangings will look the most elegant in your homes."

Sister set up her sign:

Made by the Creative Hands of the Patients
of the East Pakistan Leprosarium

The pushing begums pulled back, faces clouding, eyes glancing around, hesitating. The memsahibs pushed forward, helping to unfurl the rugs and hangings, feeling the material and asking, "Are these washable? Will the dyes fade? Are they woven on a loom?"

I started the sale by buying a round braided blue and white rug, just right to fit on my Pakistani footstool. The pace of sales picked up briskly, the memsahibs pleased to find colorful new handcrafts. When the begums saw that the American women were not afraid to buy products made by lepers, they pushed right back in, almost overwhelming even Sister Marie with their aggressiveness. It was a Macy's sale gone mad! In the swish of a sari, everything on that table was sold, and Sister was frantically writing up orders for more, more, more.

After the sale, Sister and I found a quiet corner to drink our tea while she told me how the "conference" at the Leprosarium had brought about these beautiful items.

One of the patients had been a weaver before his fingers had become too numbed and raw to work, but he offered to teach others. It was at his suggestion that the rolls of bandaging were unraveled, dyed and woven or braided into useful articles.

"Now that we have money as a result of all these sales, we can buy our much needed bandages and medicines. Isn't it wonderful, Mrs. Joy? We have a viable cottage industry to give our people a future!" She wiped tears from her round cheeks with a huge red bandana.

"I must hurry back to share the news of the good sales," she said. Then, with a sly grin, "but I'll be back soon with more beautiful items...for you to help me sell."

CHAPTER 19 OL' NO NOSE

"Look over there, Sister." I pointed to a mossy brick wall near the Sari Shop in old Dacca. "Isn't that Ol' No Nose lounging with that group of beggars?"

Sister poked her head out of the car window and squinted into the sun. "Yup, that certainly does look like Sunjit. I recognize them all. They are leprosy patients who come out to the dispensary for periodic examination, or treatment if they get really ill."

"Sunjit!" she called in her mega-bellow voice. She flailed her arm out the window to get his attention.

But in the time it took for the sound waves to travel across the road, every one of those men had disappeared.

"They don't want to see me," she said. "I tell them they must stop begging, and come learn a useful trade, but they don't want to hear it."

"It's embarrassing to admit, but I never thought of Ol' No Nose as even having another name," I said. "That's what everyone calls him. He is well known for his antics."

"What's that scoundrel done lately?" Sister asked.

"You know how he goes around old Dacca City scaring people by pushing his disfigured face up close to them? One look and most people dig deep in their pockets for rupees just to make him go away.

"One day a memsahib parked here at the Sari Shop to pick up some silk. She left her two little boys in the car because it was just a quick stop. The car was hot so the kids rolled the back window all the way down. Meanwhile, No Nose...uh, Sunjit, lounging by the wall, saw Mama Memsahib go into the shop. He shuffled over to the car, leaned his head into the open window to waggle his tongue and blow bubbles at the kids through the hole in his cheek.

"Mama came out of the shop in a couple of minutes, saw the backside of some ragged fellow with his head in the window of her car.

"'Get out of there!'" she screamed.

"Sunjit pulled back, turning around to waggle his tongue at her, as he stretched out his palm for alms. Stunned, the mother reached into her purse, pulled out a fat wad of rupees, and shoved them all at him.

"'Go away...Now!'" she scolded at him.

"He scurried off before she could realize how much she had given him. She was very angry at the leper. The boys were being much too quiet in the back seat, and she was afraid that his actions and appearance would leave them with indelible trauma.

"As they drove home, she searched for just the right words to help them understand about his disease so that they would feel compassionate, not fearful.

"Suddenly, Johnny broke the silence with, 'See, Billy? That's why Mama said we shouldn't pick our noses.'"

Sister Marie snorted. "Kids sure do have their own perspective, don't they? The problem with Sunjit and the other lepers who beg for a living is that they developed their begging skills early in their disease. They couldn't go to school, and they were never taught a trade. Many doctors have offered to give them plastic surgery, or do other surgical procedures. But the beggars refuse. Sunjit says, 'If I get a pretty face, no one will give me rupees, and I will starve.'"

As we sat in the car waiting for the stalled traffic to move, Sunjit sidled up to Sister's window.

"Salaam, Sista."

He stuck his tongue out through the hole in his cheek, waggled it rapidly, and dodged away cackling, before "Sista" could grab his arm.

She shook her head, "Even a pretty new face wouldn't help that reprobate."

PART TWO

Borders are scratched across the hearts of men
By strangers with a calm, judicial pen,
And when the borders bleed we watch with dread
The lines of ink across the map turn red.

-Marya Mannes
Subverse: Rhymes for Our Times, 1959

CHAPTER 20 **"TUNDA" IN THE MOUNTAINS**

"We are arrive, Sahibs, Memsahibs," announced Andrajhit, our guide.

"We" were a group of four friends, taking a break from the pressures of living and working in East Pakistan. Our vacation spot was Kashmir. This luxuriant high valley between India and Pakistan was an area of on-going disputes between the Hindu Indians and the Muslim Pakistanis. There had been no reports of fighting recently between the two countries, so we seized the opportunity for a visit.

Andrajhit was announcing our arrival at a camp above the valley, where we were to get horses and more guides for a side trip up to the glacier.

"We will have lunch in mountain house at glacier, where the view of Namba Parbat is most bee-ootiful! Bring warm coat," he warned. "Remember glacier, ice. Cold!"

Only at the last minute had I remembered to grab a jacket, it being so hot in the valley that I had put on my gauziest cottons.

"Memsahib, your horse." A four-legged skeleton with tufts of brown hair sagging over tyrannosaurus spines gazed at me with sad brown eyes set deep in cavernous sockets.

"Meet Geronimo, fine and noble steed to carry you up mountain's side to glacier."

I was too stunned to speak.

"Memsahib ask for slow horse. Geronimo slowest horse."

I stuttered, "Uh...do you have something a little stronger? A mule, perhaps?"

"No, Memsahib. You request slow. This is it!"

True, I had asked for a slow careful animal because my horseback riding experience had been meager and long ago. But this fellow—I should be carrying him!

However, not being one to let a puny horse with stabbing vertebrae keep me from a great adventure, I allowed myself to be shoveled atop my grand steed, only one thin horse blanket between my backside and this bony beast.

As we started up the trail, we took on the look of a cavalcade: four *ferengis*, foreigners, on our four horses; Andrajhit and three other guides walking ahead of us; and six ragged beggar-type fellows straggling along behind.

"Andrajhit!" I called, "Who are those men following us?"

As tourists, we were used to being followed, but mostly by noisy little boys vying with each other for our attention. Those "extras" were silent. They did not beg. In fact, they pretended not to notice us, but they always stayed close behind. Their presence gave me the creeps.

The guide came close to me to whisper loudly, "Espies, Memsahib." He flipped his head toward the tag-alongs. "Many espies around us. Ask no questions. Espeak only of birds and bees."

We started our climb single file, with me astride ol' Geronimo, bringing up the rear. He slipped and slid, kicking up rocks in the dry ravine that had become our trail. Misty clouds hung low in the sparse trees. I felt a shiver run up the horse's back. In the distance, I could hear a low rumble, followed by loud bursts of noise.

"What was that booming sound, Andrajhit?" I asked, now a shiver tracing my spine.

"Not to worry, Memsahib. Only *tunda* in the mountains, I am tinking."

The air was getting chill. Sprinkles were spattering my horse's head. Water began to gurgle over the rocks in our ravine trail. Soon the ragged wool horse blanket, now soaked with rain, was rubbing like sandpaper on my thinly clad thighs. The rain became tiny ice chips that grabbed at my face and clung to my yak-hair jacket.

With fingers as stiff as plaster casts, I clenched the horse's reins, determined not to fall off. Poor Geronimo, stiff-legged and quivering, got frequent jabs from the guide to hurry him along. But he continued to plod on, slipping and sliding, at the same numbed pace.

We were all hunching against the storm, sucking crystallized air into our lungs. Still, up and up we went. I scrunched my eyes to keep out the cold, but kept peeking, in case our lovely warm mountain house might be in sight.

We were all shaking by the time Andrajhit called a halt. "The lodge," he announced. "See?"

We could barely see it through the driving rain, and then, could hardly believe what we were viewing. Andrajit's "lodge" was not much larger than an outhouse. It had no windows—not even a half moon over the door.

"Soon we will have warm fire, hot tea, lunch," our guide assured us.

Desperately cold and dripping with misery, all four tourists and all four guides squeezed into the frigid shack that was our mountain shelter. It wasn't long before even our company of "espies" came in from the cold.

No room to sit. Hardly room to stand, we squeezed in together. Andrajhit found the tiny brazier and managed to start a smidgeon of fire with a few damp horse biscuits. It was going to be a long wait for hot enough water for tea, so Andrajhit brought out our lunches—four half frozen mutton sandwiches. These we divided among our four guides, our six spies, and ourselves—and like the loaves and fishes, everybody got a bite. Conversation was near to impossible because our jaws locked around the congealed mutton fat. Mostly, we stayed huddled in silence.

Suddenly, BOOM BOOM very near. BOOM BOOM. That was not thunder. Definitely not thunder!

The six spies exploded out of the doorway, three of the four guides hurtling after them.

Andrajhit barked, "Put out fire. I go. You stay. I return."

He came back shortly, commanding, "We will go now. Quickly. War!"

Forget cold. Forget thirst. Forget burning thighs. We scrambled out of the warming hut and into piles of freshly falling snow. The horses were stomping and shaking their manes.

Geronimo rose nobly to the occasion. He stumbled and slid down the gushing ravine trail, despite legs rigid with frost. I was riding on his neck, gripping the wiry hairs of his mane, praying that an extra-large jolt would not send me flying over the top of his head.

With the rapid downward speed of our slides and lurches, we soon began to defrost in the warm air of the lower hills. I could feel a slight bounce in Geronimo's steps as I slid off his neck and back onto the sopping horse blanket. Good old horse! We had made it together, and war or no war, I would take time to see that he got extra oats.

My friends had already paid off the guides, and were running for the waiting taxi. "Hurry up, Joyce. Run! Run!" they yelled back at me.

But Geronimo was going to get his reward! I handed over extra rupees to his owner, patted my new old friend goodbye, and took off, groaning and ouching as I crab-walked down to the cab.

The hired driver careened us down the mountain road, horn blasting, brakes abandoned. At the airfield, he drove directly onto the tarmac and almost up to the one small remaining plane. An airline steward rushed down its steps, both hands held out in front of him.

"Go back!" he yelled. "No more room on this plane."

The driver backed off the runway, stopping at the edge of the airfield while we considered our options. If we couldn't fly out of Srinagar, this airport, it might be possible to go by taxi to the border of West Pakistan—safe territory. But we had been warned that part of that road was unpaved and very dangerous. By the time we could make it to the border, it would be closed and we would be stuck in India.

Robert, the most travelled of our group said, "It looks like our best option is to try to bull our way on to that airplane."

He pulled from his carry case a piece of paper with an impressive-looking university letterhead. He scribbled out a couple of short paragraphs which he signed with an unreadable signature. Then he folded the letter neatly and slipped it into a long envelope on which he printed To Whom It May Concern.

"I used a letter like this once in Africa," he said, "when I was in a tough spot and had to get out of the country fast. It worked because the official could not read cursive English. If you are all willing to give this a go, we can sweeten the pot with what's left of our Indian rupees to improve our chances for getting on that plane."

The rupees we stuffed into the envelope made a generous package for any poorly paid government official, underhanded as it was. I knew that a lot of business in Asia got done this way.

Unfortunately for me, I spied the Airport Manager sign first, so I was elected to carry the letter. I took a deep breath, grabbed the packet and headed toward his office. People were milling around outside the building, or hunkering near his doorway, but no one seemed to be queuing up, so I knocked lightly.

The door was slightly ajar. I stuck my head in and cleared my throat.

"Excuse me, Sir," I said to a man behind a desk at the far end of the room.

He made a growling sound, didn't look up, continuing to stare at some papers on his desk.

"Sir," I said, speaking slowly in case he didn't understand English very well. "My three friends and I have been vacationing in your beautiful country. We are Americans, working in Pakistan. We understand that the border will be closing soon. We need your help to get us back to Pakistan before it closes. Please, Sir, will you help us?" I laid the envelope down in front of him.

The manager, impeccably groomed in stiff white shirt and dark suit, his hair slicked down with pomade, looked up. He gave me the once-over, his mouth curving downward as he stared. He said nothing. Didn't even offer tea or any of the other usual amenities that go along with any business in any office in Asia.

I glanced down at my sloppy appearance and muttered, "Horseback ride. Glacier. Rain. Sleet. Snow. BOMBS."

He nodded slightly, rocking his shoulders as he eyed the packet. With a slow deliberate move, he pulled it close to him, frowning as he glanced at the letter. With a "hmph!" he slammed it down, yanked out the wad of rupees, and flipped through them. Then he tossed them onto the desk with a sneer.

"Madam," he said, in clipped Indian English, "You are out of line. I do not approve of *bakshish*. And your letter means nothing to me. Phah!" Specks of spittle flew onto the desk.

I shriveled. My face flamed. This man was holding the key to our safety, and he had been insulted.

"I'm so very sorry, Sir," I stammered. "Is there anything..?"

The airport official heaved himself upward, his corpulent belly overflowing onto the desk.

He cleared his throat majestically as he glowered down at me. "Despite this insult, as a gracious courtesy to your gov'ment, I will give permission for your group to take this, probably the last flight, out of Kashmir, *INJA*. Give this permit to the pilot." He tossed a signed, stamped square of paper at me, and growled, "Go!"

The packet of "insult" remained on his desk.

"Thank you, thank you." I was practically gurgling with relief.

I tried not to waddle out of the room, but my chafed thighs were making me walk like a bowlegged cowboy. I could feel the eyes of that officious manager burning into my backside.

He let out a hoot. "I can see that you are the fool who got stuck with old Geronimo this time. You live in Pakistan, you deserved him!"

Furious, I straightened up, gritted my teeth and kept walking as fast as possible, afraid he would change his mind.

The exchange at the manager's office had taken too long, and my friends were about ready to send re-enforcements when I showed up. They were as glad to see me, with the permit, of course, as I was to sit down.

The taxi screeched its wheels back onto the tarmac and right to the waiting plane. We rushed up the steps, handed over the permit and flopped into the last available seats. Well, I did not flop, rather I gratefully lowered myself into a seat.

With white knuckles and held breaths, we prayed the over-loaded plane into lift-off, and safety.

CHAPTER 21 **"THIS MEANS WAR"**

September 6, 1965

"Memsahib, come now! Radio say our President espeak important message."

It's Kobad's insistent tone of voice and trembling words that sound enough of an alarm to take me away from my leisurely breakfast on the front verandah. Had it been Jahir Bux demanding, "Come now!" I would have been slug-slow to move. But Kobad never demands.

I hurry to the dining room. Jahir Bux is waving his pudgy right arm overhead, fist clenched. He scowls at the short-wave-band radio as though the news it brings is the radio's fault.

Pakistan's president, Ayub Khan, is saying, "I repeat ... India has shelled Lahore. This act of aggression means WAR!"

He slips back into Urdu, a West Pakistani language none of our Bengali servants, nor I, understand. We continue to listen, hoping for English or Bengali translation but all we get now is grating static. Kobad goes back to his brass-polishing duties, moaning, shaking his head, frowning deeply. Jahir Bux, militant and defiant, stomps outside to talk to the chowkidar.

I return to the verandah and my cold coffee. War! So ironic. I had just been thinking how comforting the familiar voices of the city had become to me. Even the high nasal chant of the muezzin calling the faithful to prayer...five times a day!...once so jarring, now seems re-assuring in its insistent regularity. I have been feeling pretty lucky, thinking about how my friends and I got out of Kashmir, *"Injá"* before the border with Pakistan shut down: poor old Baggy Bones Geronimo; Indrajit's *"tunda"* that was really bombs; the wild race back down the mountain to the airport, and out, despite our foolish attempt at bribery. Some kind of skirmish was happening there, but it doesn't really hit me until now that subversive Pakistani militants were the likely instigators of the fracas. The bombs, "tunda," were probably Pakistani. And India is retaliating.

Ever since 1947, when India gained independence from Great Britain, and Indian states that were more Muslim than Hindu were partitioned off to become a new Islamic nation, the beautiful, coveted state of Kashmir had been an area of conflict between the two countries. Kashmir was, and still is mostly Muslim, but India has held onto it as one of their states. Pakistan feels that Kashmir should belong to them. The Kashmiris are conflicted. They want a plebiscite.

"Memsahib," the chowkidar calls to me from the front gate, "See new strongest lathi to protect Sahib, Memsahib, Chota Sahib from evil India soldiers! Ashok Ali, bravest chowkidar."

He holds up a long metal pole that has a sharp stabbing point, then stomps it down hard enough to flick up bits of moist earth. He beams, whacks his bare heels together, gives me a quick salute before marching away to fend off the as-yet unseen enemy.

A battered rusty truck rattles past the front gate, red dust flying off its load of bricks. Several young boys perched atop the bricks see me. They wave the green branches they have been wearing on their heads. *"Pakistan Zindabad!"* they shout, as the truck lumbers on down the road.

Chota Sahib Steve shows up, home early from school. "Hey, Mom, did you know there is a war on? I heard some jets. East Pakistan has only three airplanes." He races for the stairs leading up to the roof, "I'll let you know if I count any extra planes."

The telephone jangles. It's Sahib. The American Consul has advised all expatriates to leave their offices, keep a low profile and stay out of sight. Sahib will be bringing three visiting consultants home.

"Kobad," I call, "please find Jahir Bux. Three guests will be here for lunch."

"Hahgee, Memsahib, I will look. But Jahir Bux angry man. I am thinking maybe he goes to join the army."

Yeah, sure...I can just see our obese cook waddling left-right, left-right, the sergeant calling "Company halt!" but Jahir Bux still lolloping forward, marching to his own stubborn tune.

Just as Sahib and the guests arrive, so does Jahir Bux from the back garden.

We all hear Steve calling from the top of the stairs, "Too many planes, Mom!"

Without even an "Excuse, please," Jahir Bux pushes a guest out of the way as he leaps for the stairway to go count airplanes.

Soon we are all shouting support to our three buzzing Pakistani jets as they chase and dive at the baddy Indian invader. It's like watching rice birds pestering a Harris hawk. We point and laugh, shouting *"Pakistan Zindabad!"* until the planes fly out of view. Lunch remembered, we trail downstairs, turn on the radio for war news while we wait for food. Only the local propaganda is broadcasting this afternoon, the announcer saying, "Pakistan Airforce has knocked out 56 Indian planes so far! The Indian government is consoling the people by saying that these were only old planes, anyway."

Christopher, a British consultant and one of our lunch guests, paces the living room floor. He picks up my bric-a-brac items and puts them back down or slips them into his pocket, his fingers feeling at the lumps they make. He peeks into corners of the room, or edges over to the curtained window for a furtive look. The room becomes quiet. The radio has been turned off.

Suddenly he shouts, "Who turned off the radio? We need to know what is going on. What is the matter with you people? Get BBC. They will tell us the true state of the war!"

We turn on the radio to appease him, waiting out the two hours of static until BBC news comes on.

We huddle around the radio to hear the British announcer say, "The East Pakistan port of Chittagong has been bombed by Indian military planes. Damage has not yet been assessed."

Kobad and Jahir Bux grab each other and wail. "Oh, Memsahib, what will become of us! So much suffer. So much suffer. Too very bad, this war!"

Several more of the expat consultants have filtered in during the afternoon and are now sitting around, casually sipping their drinks and telling ridiculous war stories. They are making light of the "great Chittagong bombing." But one engineer from the group reminds them that if India's planes hit their target, East Pakistan's only port would be knocked out of commission. Such an event would undoubtedly escalate the present skirmish, all flights would be cancelled. We would be totally hemmed in.

Up to now, I haven't even thought about that possibility. I can't envision our being in danger, nor do I think that India is in any danger from Pakistan, only 18 years a new nation, and one still divided and disorganized. All the same, I hate that our son, Doug is in enemy territory. The American International School in New Delhi is probably the safest place in India because that school is attended by many children belonging to important world-wide diplomats. At the first whiff of realistic danger, every foreign kid in that school will be whisked away to a safe location like Singapore or the Philippines. Doug is probably safer there than Steve is here. Still, I worry.

September 7, 1965

We are wakened by the sounds of jets. Again we run up to our flat roof to count four planes diving and dodging through the big fluffy thunder clouds. We watch, shocked, as an Indian jet plummets to earth near the area of Tongi, a suburb of Dacca.

Kobad calls to me a few minutes later, "Memsahib, Orphanage man come."

Salim, the charity collector for the local children's orphanage, which is situated in Tongi, stands in the doorway. He fawns at my feet and whines, "Please, please to give much rupees. Bombs kill our childrens. They break our buildings. What are we to do? You weel give much rupees today."

"Salim, there hasn't been time to assess the damage. How do you know harm was done to the Orphanage, or that any children were hurt?"

"Oh, I know, Memsahib! Bad Hindu Indians want to keel our childrens because they are Muslim."

I give him rupees. "This is to help the children. Remember, for the children—not for Salim."

The corners of his mouth make downward wrinkles in his dark face. His chin up, he looks at me sideways. With heavy tone of insulted pride he says, "Always for the orphans! Thank you," and he tromps down the steps and back out the gate.

Consul General Bowles calls a meeting for 10 a.m. of all American expats, and other foreigners who work for American companies in East Pakistan. He tells us that all commercial flights have been cancelled. Also, the Port of Chittagong has sufficient damage to prevent ships from coming in to pick us up. The American government will try to find a way to evacuate its government employees, but cannot promise to have room for others who want to leave.

"Follow black-out rules for your houses and auto lights; conserve kerosene, gasoline, and all other supplies," the Consul's aide reminds us. "Put as much as you can into storage, and pack only one suitcase each. Be ready for evacuation at any time."

Day after day we wait. It's quiet in the skies above the city now. The only threat we face seems to be the possibility of riots and jihads, Hindus against Muslims or Muslim sects against each other.

There is a pounding at my door, then a call. It is the chowkidar, pressed flat against the wall, his new lathi held in front of his face.

"What is the problem, Ashok Ali?"

"Look! Look! Men hitting at gate." He jerks his head toward the road. "Demand to talk to Sahib."

"Didn't you tell them that Sahib is not home? I will go see what they need."

"No, No! Memsahib, they will keel you!"

I walk down the driveway toward the gate, smiling and greeting them (my heart getting extra exercise). I can hear Ashok Ali trailing behind at a safe distance.

"Good morning, Young Men. My sahib is not home this morning. What can I do for you?"

"Too much sorry, Memsahib. You have hired an unbrave chowkidar. We only came to warn you to stay in your compound today. Jihad is marching. They yell and pound sticks but they mean no harm to you. Only a few find excuse to cause trouble. It is better you stay indoors. That is all."

They march on, calling out with their teen-age changing voices, "*Pakistan Zindabad!*"

More days of waiting. We expats in the neighborhood try to relieve the boredom by gathering at each other's homes for evening card games, dancing, story-telling—anything to pass the long hours. There are constant reminders from the American Consulate that

Pakistan is at war, and we foreigners must keep a low profile. It doesn't feel like war to us. Whatever is happening, like sea action near Karachi or Indian parachutists trying to land along the Punjabi border, is a thousand miles away from East Pakistan. This is just a waste of time for us here in Bengal, waiting to be evacuated from an area that doesn't appear to be in jeopardy.

Even though it doesn't feel like war to us, I find Kobad, Jahir Bux and the other servants in a huddle of whispers and hand wringing many times during the day. Kobad goes about his work with slow hands and mournful face.

Sometimes he says to me, "Memsahib, what will happen to us when you leave? We will have no jobs. No one will help protect us from the Indian soldiers when all of you are gone. We are too very much afraid."

It is hard for me to console him when I don't know what is going to happen any more than he does. But it seems to me that he is over-reacting.

The tedium of boring played-again and again games is grating on our little party group this particular evening. In the house the air is stuffy. Petty arguments start over who begins the game first or why that guy took the last cracker when this guy didn't get any—on and on. Outside, the air is delicately tropical, and the city feels safely quiet.

Suddenly, Bob, our self-proclaimed leader, stands up in front of the group and announces, "I think we should take a drive out to the Narayangang bridge. We are going stir-crazy in here. Let's all pile into two cars, lights on dim, driving with caution. Once out of the city we'll feel a lot better!"

Each one of us knows that to leave our compounds, especially at night, will be disobeying orders, and may be dangerous. Perhaps that's what makes it exciting, because we pile in on top of each other like a bunch of teen-agers after a football game. Carefully, though, with lips buttoned, we drive through the city. The auto lights are muddied to hide them from overhead view. Traffic is minimal and almost patient. Street beggars, usually so vocal and pushy, are huddling together in small anxious clusters. No bright lights. No blaring horns. No shouting hawkers. Eerie!

The air of the open countryside smells of frangipani blossoms. Tiny oil lamps are beginning to wink in the dusk. The heavy cloak of war has been left behind.

A few miles south of Dacca we come to the old bridge. "Everybody out!" Bob shouts.

I'm feeling guilty, afraid villagers will come pressing around us like they usually do, curious and suspicious. But when no one shows up, I drop my guilt into the splashing river below, and start to harmonize with the other eight, who are working on a fractured facsimile of "Shine On Harvest Moon." We are an international bunch, representing England, Norway, Germany, America, and we don't care that we don't know each other's songs, or how bad we sound. We sing with hearts feeling free, like prison escapees.

We are all standing at the middle of the bridge's span, baying at the moon's eyelash when I realize that Bob's full rich baritone voice is not among our lesser ones.

"Bob," I call, "where are you?"

He answers from a distance at the end of the bridge. "Goin' swimming."

This scares me. The night is shadowy. The undergrowth is bound to be heavy. The water still flows fast from the recent monsoons. And worse, no water in Bengal is without serious contamination from human wastes.

I'm a lot older than he, and sometimes he listens to me, so I yell, "Don't do that, Bob. Come back up. It isn't safe down there!"

"Ah, he'll be OK," one of the fellows says, "just a nature call, I'll bet."

But he does not come right back.

After ten or so minutes, and still no Bob, everyone is leaning over the railing, shouting, "Bob, you all right? Better come back now!"

Finally we hear his muffled response, "Comin' right up! NOT ALONE!"

CHAPTER 22 **CASE CLOSED**

Out of the darkness at the end of the weathered old bridge we can hear mumbled voices and the swoosh of reeds and bushes being slashed. Then a harsh "*Ek-do, Ek-do, Ek-do*" called in rhythmic cadence.

Bob's hefty figure swings up onto the bridge, followed by a company of ragged Bengali soldiers. They are butting him forward with their rifles.

Christopher, who has been bending over the railing, comes upright with a gasp. He strides toward the advancing group bellowing, "What do you think you are doing? I am British, and I say you must let this fellow go. NOW!"

"Shut up, Chris!" Bob yells, as soldiers butt at him more fiercely.

Three of the Bengalis rush forward to tussle Christopher back to our group. We others cluster together like frightened chickens in a hen house. I'm too shaken for any bold action of my own.

In fact, I'm thinking that I need to wake up. This is not a good dream.

The sergeant gestures with his gun for us to form a circle. We quickly oblige, facing each other in a broad formation. The sergeant growls a Bengali word that sounds like "boshun." I think it means "to sit" but before I can be sure that's what he is saying, a rifle butt jabs my back, and the soldier behind me shouts, "Es-sit! Es-sit!"

Now I know this is no dream. I sit!

A guard pokes at Chris's back. Chris jerks forward, yelling, "get that thing away from me. You can't do this to me. I am British!"

A gun butt cracks hard against his t-shirted back, as his attending soldier grunts, "Es-sit!"

Chris sits, stretching his legs fully forward. But he glowers up at his captor.

Heinrich, a German engineering consultant, plants his short, sturdy legs wide apart, and crosses his arms firmly. He says nothing, but he doesn't move until a squeaky-voiced Bengali squeals, "Sahib-man, to sit!"

The soldier pokes at Heinrich's backside with unquestioned determination. Clenching his fists and muttering guttural German curses, Heinrich squats in a Bengali hunker, knees deeply bent and wide apart, his backside scraping the bridge's surface. The soldier, appeased, stops poking.

Lars, next in the circle, had arrived from his home in Norway only yesterday. It's the first time out of his own country and he is taking no chances. He plops to the ground and pleads, "I don't do anyt'ing. Do not hit me. I do not even know dese people." He hunches, preparing to be beaten, but the soldier just kicks him with his heavy sandal.

We remaining captives, all Americans, are seated; silent, wary, waiting for whatever is to happen next. Now that we're all down, the sergeant calls his guards over to him to discuss our fate. My legs and back ache from sitting cross-legged for so long, but I'm too scared to move.

Bob leans forward, speaking in an undertone, "I'm sorry, Everybody. I know this is my fault. I was in the shallows under the bridge answering 'Mother Nature's call' when these soldiers found me. The sergeant insists that I am a bomb-planting spy, and that you must be spies, too, making noise to divert attention from me."

"Bloody 'ell!" Chris grabs at Heinrich's arm and says, "I say we should make a break for it!"

"Don't be fools," Bob growls. "We don't have guns. They do! No one needs to get shot here. Just stay calm, and let me handle this with the sergeant."

I know that Bob could probably sell this bridge to nomads in the Sahara Desert. So if this sergeant can understand enough English—and the Pakistani military law is not a "take no prisoners" policy (gulp)—I'm pretty sure that he will get us out of this terrifying situation. He's keeping much cooler than I am feeling.

Bob stands up slowly, his arms raised high over his head. He calls to the sergeant, who stalks toward the circle with his rifle pointing directly at Bob's chest.

The guards hurry back to us, their prisoners. My boy pokes his rifle butt between my shoulder blades to let me know he's there. I look back and give him a hint of a smile, trying not to show how creepy his presence makes my skin feel.

Away from the circle, alone with the sergeant, Bob gestures and points, trying to make the Bengali man understand. His tone of voice is rising with frustration.

'Keep cool, Bob. Keep cool,' I am thinking. 'We don't need any jumpy villagers to know we're here. Bengalis tend to be excitable under stress, and having experienced war in the past, their panic could put us in serious trouble—as though we aren't already.'

It is hard not to whisper among ourselves but we don't dare to agitate our captors. It would take only one little finger slip to make a mass murder, even without extra villagers.

Agonizingly long minutes later, the sergeant calls four soldiers over to surround Bob, who is allowed to take the car keys out of his pocket. Then the guards march him back to the circle to tell us what has been decided, and to hand the keys to Doc.

"I have agreed to go to the Cantonment with the sergeant. The rest of you are free to leave, but that means you must go directly home! These soldiers are staying here to guard the bridge. The sergeant and I, in the Army truck, will follow your cars through the city. Doc, you will need to let Habib know where I am—and please, nobody mention this incident, or we could all be in big trouble. See ya tomorrow."

No one talks as we climb into the two cars. We're nothing like we were when this adventure began—a bunch of freedom freaks.

Once we are safely away, I blow out a "Whew! What a relief to get away from those soldiers. It isn't fair for Bob to take the blame for us, though. We all chose to come out here. We are equally guilty."

The others nod, and Doc says, "I'll drop you at the house and go find Habib right away. Let's hope that he can convince the Pakistani military interrogators to release Bob, before they rough him up too much."

I have new appreciation for this young ex-farmer who calmly defused a potentially deadly situation. Whatever he said to the sergeant convinced the man to let the rest of us go. Otherwise, we would all be where Bob is.

I have much faith in Habib, too. His Genii lamp can make Pakistani problems poof away. That, plus his large *bakshish* budget.

Safely back home, we spend most of the night in subdued discussion about the "bridge event," as we call it in secret reference. Personally, I'm so ashamed of having been a part of it that I never want to talk about this night again.

It has taken this incident to make me realize that this is not a comic war, but a conflict between two nations, each ready to kill to get its own way. The Pakistanis understand this because only eighteen years ago they lived through the bloody transition of becoming a new nation. Many lost their entire families. Complete village populations were murdered. Their lives were so disrupted that they are only now beginning to cope. Both Jahir Bux and Kobad recall those days with horror. Now I understand why they are so frightened about this new conflict.

"I'm starving. What's for breakfast?" Bob bounds in the back door, calling in a jaunty voice.

If I didn't know where he'd been last night, I would have thought he'd been on a week's bender. His wavy brown hair is flying in every direction, dark circles underline his green eyes, the right sleeve of his t-shirt is half-torn away.

"What happened to you, Bob?" Everyone questions him at once but he keeps his mouth full of scrambled eggs and slurps of hot coffee.

Finally, he looks up from his well-cleaned plate, and says, "Nothing happened. Nothing at all. This case is closed!"

He holds his right index finger up to his lips.

Habib and his Genii lamp have come through again.

CHAPTER 23 TIME TO FLY

SEPTEMBER 19, 1965

It's 7:00 a.m. I've just downed my last bite of breakfast papaya.

"Memsahib, America Consulate driver bring letter for you." Tears are rolling down Kobad's face as he hands me a sealed envelope. "I know what means this, Memsahib. You and Chota Sahib and Sahib go away now—not come back." His shoulders shake as he sobs. "What to do! What to do!"

"Not to worry, Kobad. Sahib will be staying right here. You and Jahir Bux will need to take care of him. Chota Sahib and I want to stay, too, but our government says we must go. It will be your responsibility to take good care of Sahib while we are gone. Will you do that for me, please?"

Kobad beams. "Oh, yes, Memsahib! Thank you, Memsahib!"

He mops his face with his shirttail as he hurries off to tell Jahir Bux the good news.

"Grab your gear, Steve. This is it," I say, waving the Consulate directive.

We had been warned that we must be ready on very short notice. But one hour! Steve squashes in as much extra stuff as his already full bag will hold. My bag is packed, but I race around to collect medical supplies and containers of boiled water. I'm the designated "flight nurse" for the plane we will be on.

"Oh, toilet paper! Steve, would you mind carrying these three rolls?"

"Ah, Mom. They're pink!"

"OK, you carry the jugs of water. I'll do the t.p."

At the car, the servants are lined up in a neat row, just as they were when we first came to Dacca. This time there are no smiles, no salutes, just sober salaams.

Steve gets a worried look, and says, "We are coming back, aren't we, Mom? I want Dad and my friends, especially Andy, to help me finish building my dinghy."

I give him a squeeze, sopping some of my own tears onto his shirt, and trying to reassure him.

"We certainly will come back as soon as our government will let us."

Dacca isn't an easy place to live. Steve has adjusted much faster than I have. He has his pet mongoose, and his boat kit to work on, and his buddies at school. The soggy tropical heat hasn't seemed to bother him much, as it has me. It has taken me a long time to get used to the batch of all-male servants I am supposed to be supervising. But I'm learning to truly appreciate the uniqueness of this land, and I'm not ready to leave it.

At the Consulate, so many ex-pats are milling around, talking loudly, crying and waving goodbyes, that it takes several major raps with a gavel to quiet the room enough for Mr. Bowling to speak. He tells us that we will be given numbers which represent the plane on which we will be flying. At the airport, we are to join the group which represents our number. He urges us to remain calm, wishes us all the best on our journey, and hopes to see us back again after the hostilities have ceased.

At Dacca International Airport, the first United States Air Force plane has just landed.

"Look at the size of that plane, Mom!" Steve gasps.

A man standing nearby tells us that it is a C-130, a cargo plane. It looks like a huge guppy. We watch the first group of evacuees struggle up the steps, dragging their bulging suitcases. The door slams shut and plane #1 roars down the runway for lift-off. Our plane, #2, is already circling for landing.

The man who assigned our group gathers all seventy of us. "People, it is important for you to move as fast as you can as soon as you are called to board, so that your plane can take off, and plane #3 can land. For the safety of all, this evacuation *MUST* be done quickly!"

My heart is pumping madly. I feel like turning around and running away fast, very fast. But the Consulate assigner points me out to the group. "Your Consulate nurse will be your flight nurse. She has air-sick pills, vomit bags and some other medications, and some drinking water. If you have questions, please ask her. The pilots will be too busy to be disturbed."

"Are we flying directly to The Philippines?" someone shouts.

"No, the first leg of the trip is to Bangkok, Thailand, with about six hours of lay-over."

Others crowd around with questions. I hope they get all the answers they need because if I'm supposed to give them answers, they'll be out of luck. I haven't been told anything more than anyone else. Having been reminded of my responsibility, I feel my panic dissipate.

Our plane lands. We hurry up the ramp. Steve is bouncing with excitement, but I feel like I'm entering the bowels of the beast. I'm sad. I'm scared. And then, I'm shocked. This plane is no luxury Pan Am.

"Look, Mom, there aren't any seats! We have to sit in these hammock nets, just like the soldiers do." Steve looks around the plane's enormous cavity. "Where do you suppose the 'head' is?"

"I'm looking for it, too," I answer. "I'd like to put this toilet paper somewhere other than on my lap."

Dick, a school friend of Steve's, points to a narrow blue-plastic curtained area, and shouts in his loud pre-teen voice, "I'll bet that's the pot, where everybody can see it."

Dick is right. It isn't exactly private, but we will at least have pink toilet paper—while it lasts.

People are trying to fit down into the heavy hammock netting, their belongings tucked under their feet. The seating is uncomfortable and we are jammed together. Overhead, a big dome of space is already filling with the roar of the great plane's engines.

"Everybody, strap in. We are about to take off," the pilot shouts over the loud speaker.

With a bone-rattling roar, we are racing down the runway, and beginning the lift-off. Light is very dim inside the plane, and with no windows at seat level I feel like I'm in the stomach of a prehistoric animal. Several small children grab their mommies, and hang on tight, but nobody panics.

Although the flight is smooth, the extreme noise presses heavily. Five hours of sitting in the netted seating with its lack of good back support makes the trip seem much longer. I dispense a lot of aspirin. One of the ladies sitting close to me is near to term in her pregnancy. I get pretty anxious when her wild two-year old starts jumping up and down on his mama's remaining bit of lap. This is no place to deliver a baby.

Our plane arrives in Bangkok before any of the others. As we stumble down the ramp, we are amazed to see a *WELCOME TO BANGKOK* sign waving at us. Then, shouts of greeting by a contingent of friendly Americans, who lead us to hot coffee and doughnuts. I am embarrassed at their solicitousness when I hear that many of our greeters had themselves been evacuated from Viet Nam.

The respite has been sweet, but when our flight is called we stoically line up to board our #2. It is already 6:00 pm, and we have many more hours to fly.

"If this flight is as smooth as the flight from Dacca," I say to Steve, as we walk toward the plane, "maybe we can catch a nap."

A blocky man in a sharp-looking Air Force uniform is standing near the ramp.

"That doesn't look like our pilot," Steve points out. "In fact, that's a...Mom, that's a general!"

The man reaches out his hand to grasp Steve's for a handshake. "I am General Stillwell," he states in a loud, confident voice. "I do not anticipate that this skirmish will last very long. You will be back in Dacca in no time. So relax and enjoy the rest of your flight."

He sounds so sure of himself, I almost believe him, all but the "relaxing" part. It is, after all, the same plane, the same seating and crowding together. But the lighting seems even dimmer, the roaring even more ear-blasting. As we get underway the air feels heavy and chill.

Suddenly, there is down-drop, then an extra great roar, and we are lifting fast. All the lights are doused, inside the plane and out. We are hitting giant pockets of turbulent air, causing us to bump hard against each other. People are coughing and vomiting. Someone hands me a flashlight. I stagger around among the passengers, passing out extra vomit bags, and trying to give comfort. A tall man in the group stretches to look out the high window.

"I'm not sure where we are," he announces loudly, "but I can see ground flak!"

The co-pilot steps out of the cockpit to ask Steve and Dick to hand out safety jackets.

"There aren't enough jackets for all the passengers," Steve yells to the pilot. "What'll we do?"

Both pilots strip off their own safety jackets to share with two men who didn't get any.

Steve and I huddle together, tensed again for the next bump or jerk. The only light is coming from small flashlights. Even that much is comforting.

It is 2:00 a.m. The air is calmer now. A few people are slumped in exhausted sleep. Steve's head bobs against my shoulder.

Suddenly, the lights glare on, inside and out. Passengers jerk awake. I feel shocked and blinded after being in the dark for so long.

The pilot announces, "Folks, sorry to have kept you in the dark that way, but we didn't want to be seen while we were flying over 'Nam. All of our lights are on now because a reconnaissance plane following us needs to see who we are. We expect to reach Manila in approximately one hour."

We clap, we laugh, we shake hands, we hug. We don't know exactly where we'll be living, or what to expect, but the grind and the tension of this trip are almost over, and we are joyous.

PART THREE

Ours were many voices but we sang a common song
Ours were different words, diverse tunes
But our music was the same.
                    -Shahidullah Kaiser

CHAPTER 24 **PARANOIA**

After several months, the hostilities between Pakistan and India had calmed, and Steve and I had been given our government's permission to return.

Habib met us right off the plane at the Dacca Airport, and quickly hurried us through Customs.

"Welcome home, Memsahib and Steve Sahib. Sahib is on his way returning from the mofusils. His message to you is that he will be back before nightfall."

As we drove through the city we looked closely at everything, somehow expecting to see major changes. But everything appeared to be as it had been when we left—busy, noisy, dirty, with a few new buildings, and a lot of old ones. It was our same old Dacca, thank goodness!

Ashok Ali was quick to open the gate as we turned into our driveway. He gave us a proper military salute, one of his best. Outside the front verandah, the servants were again lined up to greet us.

Tears ran down Kobad's cheeks as he said, "So much welcome, Memsahib, Chota Sahib. It is good that you are home."

Jahir Bux smiled and salaamed, but he didn't echo Kobad's impassioned greeting, I suspect because he had been quite happy having full control of the household in my not-around-to-interfere absence.

I grinned at Steve and squeezed his hand. It felt good to be back. Things seemed normal, even Jahir Bux's lack of enthusiasm fit.

In many ways, things were the same as before we left. But there were a couple of odd additions. Our telephone was being tapped. Hadn't had that before. Our phone conversations were frequently interrupted with "Please to espeak more clearly."

One day our Norwegian house guest, who had a pronounced Scandinavian accent, was talking on the phone when his conversation was interrupted with a harsh, "Espeak English! I cannot to understand you."

Our insulted friend answered just as sharply, "I AM speaking English, you fool. If you are going to butt in, you had better learn the language!"

Outside our compound gate, a plain-clothes man wandered past, on to the corner, and back again past the house. At first he appeared furtive, but after a few days he dropped all pretense, to the point of even harassing our timid chowkidar. Ashok Ali no longer went outside the compound wall, but did his patrolling inside the gate. He marched back and forth, his sturdy lathi grasped firmly in hand, calling for Allah's attention in constant shrill petition.

When anyone attempted to leave or to enter our gate, the plain-clothes fellow would come with questions, like, "Where are you go? Who are your name? Why you to come to this place?"

This went on for several months, more funny than annoying. We assumed that it was just part of the general post-war paranoia until we discovered that the neighbor in the next compound to ours was a colonel in the Pakistani Army. Undoubtedly he knew the bridge story, and felt obliged to keep an eye on his neighbors, the spies.

So when Habib called me to the General Service Office one morning, I was a bit concerned. Was he going to quiz me about the never-discussed bridge incident?

"Memsahib, I am needing your assistance. A new Ford Foundation advisor will be coming for the Comilla Agriculture Project."

Eager to keep away from "that other" subject, I was quick to respond, "Great, Habib. What do you need?"

"A—um, Memsahib, a—," The smooth-talking Habib was tripping all over his words. "The living quarters in Comilla have need of repairs. So, to stay with you, hah-gee, yes, until it is ready. I very thank you—and Sahib."

This was not an unusual request, since Dacca had no Western-style hotels, and our Foundation guest house was small and often full. On similar occasions in the past, he had just telephoned to tell me what he needed. Was something different this time?

"Of course, we will be happy to welcome him," I answered.

"Them, Memsahib," Habib corrected me softly.

"Oh, his wife is coming, too? Very good."

"Also, baba—childs."

"Fun! I love kids, and you know we have plenty of room."

"Hah-gee, Memsahib." Habib beamed an Olympian-size grin, his eyes twinkling like a starry night. I felt suspicion rising in my throat.

"Okay, Habib, how many 'childs'?"

His eyes, sideways glanced, his neck giving me that Asian twist, he muttered, "Maybe...ten."

"TEN, HABIB!"

"Well, maybe not," he answered, full-force grin again, "Just testing."

I shook my head and laughed, happy that that "spy" business hadn't changed his opinion of me enough that he couldn't tease...or did he really mean 'testing'?

As I left the office, he called out, "By the way, new family coming soon...today."

Was he holding the bridge incident over my head, or was I getting paranoid, too?

CHAPTER 25 INTRIGUE IN BENGAL

"Habib!" I yelled, as I raced into the General Service Office, waving my letter. "Son, Donn, in the Peace Corps in West Bengal, has a week of leave time coming. The Government of India won't give him a permit to cross the border into Pakistan, but if I can cross from Pakistan side we could meet in Calcutta. You can arrange that for me, yes, Habib?" I stopped my frenzied talking just long enough to gasp up a big breath.

"I know that flights between India and Pakistan haven't commenced since the Kashmiri conflict, but I could fly to Khulna, take a taxi to the border, and then catch the train on India's side to get to Calcutta. You can fix that for me, can't you?"

Habib did not respond to me in his usual jovial manner. He remained seated behind his large desk, deep furrows between his brows. I had never seen him look so serious.

"Please to sit, Memsahib. Have some nimbu pani. I think you were maybe running. You need to rest." He asked his assistant to get me a glass of cold limeade. It was an obvious stall.

"My news is not good." He waggled his head. "Not to go, Memsahib. Too much danger. I cannot arrange you a permit. So sorry! So sorry!"

"But why can't you help me, Habib? You have always been here for me. You are the most obliging, most efficient, the kindest person I have met since I have been in Pakistan. I can't believe you would let me down now! The war is over, so what is the problem?"

This is the point at which Bengalis always answered, "No problem, Memsahib," whether or not there was a problem. This time Habib did not respond, "No problem, Memsahib." Instead, he waggled his head, fiddled with the papers on his desk, sighed deeply.

"Habib, please try to help me! It has been so long since I last saw my son, and now that he is in India, we have this chance to meet."

Tears slipped down my face. I blew my nose. I begged. I wheedled. Habib continued to shake his head and fumble with things on his desk, not glancing up at me.

When I realized that nothing else was working, I pulled out the big gun: name-dropping.

"Maybe," I said, bending over his desk so he had to look at me, "maybe I need to go directly to Chauduri Sahib, the Home Minister. He and Begum Chauduri had dinner with us recently. We talked a lot about our children, and their importance in our lives. He will understand how much this trip means to me."

Habib lifted his head, quieting its negative waggle. He grinned a very slight sideways grin.

"Ah, Memsahib, if a person should go directly to the Home Minister's office, a person might possibly get a permit." His dark brown eyes roamed the walls and the ceiling. "That is what I can tell you."

I understood then that some government restriction was limiting his ability to help me, so he was showing me a way to handle the request myself. If anyone knew how to find and play the angles, Habib did. It was whispered that he was a counter-spy.

I hurried over to the government office of Mr. Chauduri. He greeted me effusively, urging cup after cup of very hot, very sweet tea. As one does in these office visits, we talked of the weather, the glorious blooming trees along the boulevard, how well the children were doing in school, until, finally, he asked me why I had honored him with my visit.

I didn't flower it up the way I had seen some politicians do; didn't throw down a bribe; just flat out requested a permit to cross the Pakistan-Indian border.

He frowned and waggled his head like Habib had done, and my heart sank.

"Please, Chauduri Sahib," I said. "This opportunity to be with my son means so much to me. If anyone in Gov'ment can help me, I believe it is you."

He reached into his desk drawer, all the while shaking his head. I held my breath. He pulled out a permit, embossed it with an impressive-looking stamp, and squiggled his signature.

"You must travel cautiously," he said, as he handed me the permit. "Even though we are no longer at war, Pakistan and India are not friendly. Spies are everywhere. Be careful!"

"Oh, thank you so very much! And I do promise to be careful. When I return, you and Begum Chauduri must come for dinner, so you can hear all about my trip."

I bubbled on like an idiot as he escorted me to the office door. His smile was not much more than polite as we parted.

I felt like a puff of cloud skimming the sidewalk on my way back to the car, the permit like a feather in my hand. I wanted to wave it for all to see. But a niggling guilt began to edge into my fluff.

Most Muslim government officials would attend social functions with Westerners if it helped their agenda. I had made no pretense about what I had wanted. My request was granted because Chauduri Sahib felt obligated. It was how the "game" was played, but it gave me a very uncomfortable feeling. My poofy cloud evaporated.

Back with Habib, I handed over the permit. "I apologize for suggesting Mr. Chauduri's name in my effort to obtain this. Thank you for the gracious way you helped me to help myself."

"You know, Memsahib, that your pleasure pleases me. But, it is not a good thing for you to be doing, this traveling to Calcutta." He waggled his pointing finger at me. "If you must go, please accept help whenever it is offered. Inshallah, God willing, you will be safe."

Habib's face and his voice seemed sincerely concerned for my safety, so I promised to be very careful, and to take help if any were offered.

The airplane from Dacca to the border town of Khulna, East Pakistan was a small Fokker Friendship carrying two burka-wreathed women, three Bengali elders, whose hair was dyed a proud orange to prove they had made their *hajs* to Mecca, and myself. After a short flight, we bumped down onto the grass-tufted runway. A rusting yellow auto carrying a large TAXI sign on its roof, drove right onto the tarmac to meet us.

"Ho, Memsahib! You taxi now." A very dirty little Bengali man hopped out of the cab. He flipped off the *Hajis*, who shook their fists at the taxi driver.

"You, Memsahib, come now," his voice was a scratchy tenor, his right arm a directional windmill.

'Should I go with this guy?' I thought. 'A rattle trap vehicle and a seedy-looking driver, but those *Hajis* had been willing to ride with him, and Habib had said...and the offer of assistance was obvious.'

So, with a frog-sized lump in my throat I slid onto the rear passenger seat, careful to avoid the rusty spring sticking out through the cracking leather. A wad of rags on the seat stunk of oil. I pushed them onto the floor.

Rattle, rattle, burp, boom! We jerked ahead, whizzing past the terminal shack, taxi horn ablast. I latched onto that broken spring, the only place I could get a good grip, as Taxi man played chicken with a truck piled high with bricks. He chortled as it tipped into a ditch. When we came to an intersecting road I could see a large arrowed sign that read BORDER. Taxi man took the other road.

"Hey! You, Driver!" I yelled, as I jerked at his shoulder. "The sign shows that the border is the other way. That is where I need to go. Turn around NOW!"

"Ha gee," he grunted. "Get jack, then go."

I considered jumping out but he was not slowing down. It seemed best to wait until we were in a more populated area. And maybe he WAS just picking up a jack. I took a deep breath and tried to relax.

Just past a sharp curve, the taxi lurched to a stop in front of a battered wooden shack. Taxi man jumped out and raced behind the building. Moments later, a large man wearing a striped blue turban, strode over to the driver's seat. He folded himself behind the steering wheel. Taxi man sashayed around to the shotgun position.

"Jack," he said, with a flip of his head toward the new driver.

I had taken Taxi man on faith, but that faith had not included this guy! He was no Bengali. By the turban, the loose baggy shirt and pants he was wearing, and his large size, he was surely a Pathan tribesman from the northwest part of Pakistan. These men, known for their fierce and stealthy lifestyles, were hired as guards to protect government officials. They had the reputation as "hit men." In his home area, he would have been carrying a bandolier and Kalashnikov rifle. He didn't have them now, but I knew that in one of the many

Never Cheat A Holy Man

folds of his voluminous pants, a razor sharp kris would be tucked into its leather scabbard.

Choking down panic, I greeted "Jack" with a murmured "salaam." He nodded, jerked the taxi into squealing action, heading us back in the direction of the border. Taxi man reached over to press on the horn, honking it without let-up.

"Why you are going to India? You are spy?" Jack turned his head repeatedly to look at me, as he interrogated. "You are having lover in India? We cut off nose from such evil woman! Why you not send husband to India? You are carrying gold across border for friends? We keel such evil woman!" On and on he went, not waiting for me to answer him.

I gritted my teeth. What I wanted was for him to turn around, shut up, and watch the road. Taxi man continued to push on the horn but his attention stayed on me. We managed somehow to reach the border without running into the ditch. Allah must have been steering. No one else was.

We were still rolling to a stop when "Jack" jumped out of the car and took off. While I was getting out, Taxi man was dumping my luggage on the ground. He hopped back into the car and squirreled away, without a wave or a salaam, or even his fare. Spine tickling!

The Pakistan border guard, dressed in a neat khaki uniform with green trim, eyed my permit, turning it over and over. Then he squinted at me, asked if I had gold.

"You cannot carry gold out of Pakistan!" he told me sternly. "Why you say you have no gold? I see you have gold ring!"

"Sir!" I drew myself up as tall as possible. With my chin held high, I said "This is my marriage ring!"

"Oh, sorry, Memsahib. My mistake." He ducked his head and turned away.

The second guard opened my bag, but seeing my "unmentionables" on top, he felt around the edges of the case.

"Ah! Chocolate bar, Memsahib." He pointed to a candy bar tucked into one of the corners, and grinned broadly.

"If you like, you must have this before it melts," I said. Both of us knew this little game was a bribe, the evidence of which the guards could swallow.

The officer held the candy in one hand while he closed the suitcase lid with the other. I grabbed the case, thanked the men and walked toward the gate which separated East Bengal, Pakistan from West Bengal, India.

"Wait, Memsahib!" It was the guard who had not found the chocolate. "You do have gold. I saw you have gold teeth in mouth!"

"Yes, I do," I called back. "That's where they will stay! And no more chocolate."

I could hear the guards laugh as I walked on.

Officials on India's side of the border were dressed like those on the Pakistani side, uniforms the same, except the khaki was trimmed with red instead of green. The guards all looked similar, their builds slender, small facial features, dark coloring. They could be related. Before Partition in 1947, they would have been living side by side. Now they were on opposite sides of a border gate, a recent war, and a very shaky peace.

They casually glanced at my passport and Pakistani exit permit. "Why you want to come to India?" one guard asked. "Better country, eh?" He swaggered his shoulders, and did the Asian neck twist.

Without answering, I opened my suitcase lid. Neither fellow touched anything, but one man tipped his head in the direction of the Pakistani border station.

"I heard they got choc-o-lat." He held out his hand, an impish grin on his face.

We all laughed as I brought out the last two candy bars from around the edge of the suitcase.

As I walked away from the guard station, I noticed two bicycle rickshas standing in a clump of trees a short distance off.

'I surely hope I can get one of those,' I thought. 'Habib told me that the train station is several miles away.'

A clean-shaven young Bengali man, dressed in a hip-length shirt and loose blue jeans came out from behind one of the shade trees. He walked over to me, nodded his head and then firmly removed my bag from my hand to hurry it over to one of the rickshas.

"Stop!" I yelled, as I ran after him.

He wore a Buddha smile as he stated in excellent English, "Memsahib, you are taking the train to Calcutta. Your ricksha will follow mine." Spine tingle.

I could have protested, but to whom? The guards wouldn't care about me now that the chocolate bars were gone. Anyway, following

Habib's mantra, this fellow seemed to be the "offered help." And he was not dirty, rude, armed or dangerous, as far as I could tell.

So I climbed into the ricksha that held my bag, putting my fate in the hands of God, Allah, Habib, the Buddha guide, and the ricksha driver. That ought to be enough protection.

As we pulled up to the train station, the man who had grabbed my bag, hurried over to finally introduce himself. "I am Nirad. I will help you. Give me the rupees for your train ticket. I will buy mine at the same time. We will sit together. No problem, Memsahib."

'No problem for him,' I thought, 'but this was really stretching my faith. Had Habib meant this much help?' I took a deep breath, plunged into my purse and handed over the ticket rupees. Nirad would not have to exchange Pakistani rupees for the Indian ones, sometimes a problem getting their full value. Efficient Habib had already taken care of that.

True to his statement, Nirad and I sat together in a first class compartment. He questioned me so politely that I didn't feel like I was being interrogated, the uncomfortable way "Jack" had done, but I still recognized his questioning for what it was.

At the Calcutta station, I asked Nirad to find me a taxi cab so I could meet my son at the hotel.

"No problem, Memsahib. I will accompany you."

"No, no," I protested. "You have helped me much too much. I will be fine now." But that didn't stop him from coming along.

Never was I more pleased to see my son than when we arrived at the hotel where he was waiting at the entry. He waved his black umbrella and dashed to the taxi to keep me from getting wet. This was protection I was happy with. I turned to introduce him to Nirad, but, just like "Jack," Nirad had disappeared.

As we walked into the hotel lobby, I got a glimpse of a tall Pathan with a blue turban just like the one "Jack" had been wearing. Not too unusual, I supposed, but there was that tingle down the back again. I know the man saw me because he ducked into the elevator, and was gone.

Probably a different man. Asia tends to make one paranoid.

Donn and I had a grand visit in Calcutta, an ancient city like Dacca, but so much more sophisticated. We saw the sights, the movies, the temples, the gardens. We heard the music, ancient and modern, and smelled the smells...well, they weren't any different from

Dacca. Our visit was over too soon, of course, but Donn had to put on his Peace Corps hat again and return to the Hindu village, and I had to put on my Memsahib hat and fly back to Muslim Bengal, Pakistan.

India, just this week, had lifted the ban on Pakistani planes flying across Indian borders.

I went to the airport not knowing when I could get on a flight. There was a long line at the ticket counter.

When it was finally my turn, the agent looked at me and said, "Your name, please?"

I told him my name.

"Oh, yes, Memsahib. Here is your ticket. You may board now."

Had to be that amazing Habib, able to reach across borders. No spine tingle.

Sure enough, Habib was at the Dacca airport to meet me. "So happy to see that you are safely returned," he said. "One worries about how such trips will turn out these days."

"My trip was safe all along the way, thanks very much to you. I took your advice and accepted all obvious help."

Habib's brow wrinkled into a deep furrow. "But Memsahib, Gov'ment refused to allow me to help you!"

A full-blown shiver shot up my spine. "Then who did send those people?"

Habib grinned his familiar slant-wise smile. "Must have been Allah," he answered.

CHAPTER 26   **WEL-CUM MEMSAB**

Jahir Bux and Kobad were "cousin brothers" from the same extended family village. In moments of chattiness they had told me stories about their families, so when Kobad asked me if I would like to visit their village, I didn't feel uncomfortable with the idea.

"Everyone ask many questions about memsahib, want you to come. No memsahib has ever come to visit us."

Jahir Bux told me that he had four daughters and one son. "Daughters are very hard," he said.

"Must find husbands for them, and pay dowries. Much money. Much trouble.

"But I have one son. I thought a son would be the best. Everyone said, 'Aha, you are lucky to have a son.' But I am not lucky! This son does nothing but sit and dream and play his flute. His mother tells him to go to work in the paddy, but he does not go, even when she takes a big stick to him. He does not even go to his lessons at the mosque. What to do with such a son?"

Kobad told me that his father wants him to have a son, but as yet he has only an infant daughter.

"My wife is not strong, and I don't want her to die, as my mother did when I was born. I lived always with my aunties and grandmothers. My father never took another wife. My wife says it is because no woman would be willing to marry such a cross old man.

"He is not well. He walks with a stick. He yells at everyone, and complains about everything my wife does for him. When I go to the village, my wife scolds me because Father beats her with his stick. I talk to him but he says 'Bah! It is her duty to do as I say. She is my daughter-in-law.' What he says is true. That is our way."

Jahir Bux told me that he was born in West Bengal, near Calcutta, of a Muslim family. During Partition, when India became independent of Britain, he came with his family to East Bengal, newly named Pakistan.

"It was a horrible time, Memsahib. You cannot imagine. Hindus killed Muslims to take our land and villages, and our people did the same to the Hindus so that we would have a place to live. I can never see a train now without recalling the bloody bodies and hearing the screaming people on that train.

"Kobad's family came, too. His father's wife was killed. He later married Kobad's mother, but she died when Kobad was born. Perhaps the old man is cross because he remembers too much."

I had visited a few villages as part of my nursing job with the American Consulate, but had never had an invitation on a personal level. I was eager to meet Kobad's and Jahir Bux's families in their village, not just as characters in their stories, but as village people in their own real settings. It would be an honor to be the first Caucasian woman to visit them.

In preparation for the trip, I consulted my Bengali neighbor, Begum Halani.

"You must wear a sari and sandals like all Bengali ladies wear." She leaned in to peer at me. "You must do something about your red hair, and, Oh, my, those skin spots. The villagers may think you have a disease."

She squinted at me suspiciously. "You don't have a skin disease, do you?"

I laughed a little and shook my head. I was aware that my freckles brought comments. One woman who had stared at me in a local shop, asked me in a pitying voice, "Can't a doctor cure your warts?"

"Well, I suppose you can't help the spots, but you can dye your hair black, like all Bengali ladies have." I took her advice.

As the hair-dresser poured on the black dye she shook her head and muttered that I needed to keep the dupatta scarf over my hair at all times. I did not leave the beauty salon brimming with confidence.

Begum Halani helped me choose a gauzy green sari trimmed with gold threads on the sari end, the scarf, and the matching blouse. I bought some attractive flowered sandals with thin straps that went over the big toes to hold them to my feet. They felt firm, and since Kobad had said we would be traveling by ferry and bus, this garb should be comfortable.

When Kobad saw me in my new black hair, cool green sari and colorful sandals, he grinned shyly and exclaimed, "Memsahib look like proper begum now."

His pronouncement of me as an upper class Bengali memsahib gave me the confidence I needed to wear this outfit without embarrassing my host.

The morning of our trip was sparkling clear, and already searing the early dawn. I felt bubbly with excitement as I climbed into a bicycle ricksha. Kobad, already in his ricksha, lead the way through Old Dacca. The ricksha drivers pedaled at a reasonable pace, with much attention to their ding-ding bells, until we got into the wild traffic of the old city.

Suddenly we became major competitors in the Indi 500 of Bengal. Our rickshas darted around bullock carts, careened in and out between pedestrians with baskets of chickens on their heads, and lame old men hobbling on make-shift crutches. We tipped sideways on one wheel to skinny past a fat bus, jammed with shouting humans. A scrawny horse pulling a medieval-looking carriage reared up when my driver drove his ricksha wheel too close. Inside the carriage, a woman screamed.

I was about ready to jump to safety, when our rickshas came to an abrupt stop just short of dunking us into the grimy foam of the Burhi Ganga river, our ferry destination.

People already waiting on the shore had to jump out of our way, pushing and tripping against each other. They buzzed like a hive of angry bees as they jostled back in to gain their rights at the front. A couple of men grabbed our ricksha drivers, shaking them and threatening angrily.

Petrified, I crunched back into my seat, praying I would not be noticed. Kobad remained a sphinx of calmness, ignoring the crowd as though they were shadows.

As things quieted, he said, "Come now, Memsahib. Must to get our place."

He elbowed the grumbling crowd aside to get us to the front spot on the ferry landing. I kept my head down as much as possible, with my hair well covered.

It was a relief to be with Kobad, and to be incognito. *AMERIKIS GO HOME* signs were scrawled all over the brick walls of Old Dacca. It wouldn't take much to inflame this unpredictable mass. I watched for clues from Kobad, but he seemed perfectly at ease, so I took a deep breath and tried to relax.

What was I thinking! One was not wise to take more than sips of air in the Old City. The stink, it was said, could petrify one's lungs. Body odors fused with bullock pies and urine. Bidi cigarette smoke blended with acrid cow-dung fires. Here by the river, decaying fish stink added to the general stench. Searing heat melded the lot.

'Draw it in, or rise above it,' I thought. 'I will concentrate on observing my surroundings.'

I watched a two-man skiff with a patched square red sail slip by on the other side of the river. Two larger fishing boats with bamboo covers slid past in the fast-flowing grey water.

"Many families live aboard boats like that during monsoon season when their villages flood," Kobad said. "If they don't have boats they must come into Dacca and live on the streets."

He interrupted himself as people began to shove in around us.

"Our ferry just now coming." He pointed to an un-railed raft being poled, slant-wise, across the wide expanse of the river, a fast current tugging against it.

No other ferry-type boat was even visible so I took his word that this was the thing that would carry all of these people, their goods and animals, and the two of us, to the other side of the river.

The raft hadn't even tied up yet when people began to jump aboard, throwing their containers and live critters ahead of them. I had been eager to take this "ferry" trip, to feel the cool river breezes and to experience river travel as the Bengalis did. But I was no Tom Sawyer. I hesitated.

"Now, Memsahib, now," Kobad called.

Suddenly I was shoved forward onto the ferry, angled between a small brown goat and a woman clutching an over-sized basket. The two white geese in it took turns pecking at the freckles on my arms. All around me were women with little children, and large bundles of market goods such as bananas and mangoes.

On the outer edges of the raft were the men. They stood or hunkered with their backs to us. I could see that Kobad had joined their contest of spitting as far out from the raft as possible. I hoped the wetness that was hitting my cheeks was river water.

Every day the Dacca News reported mass drownings due to overloaded ferries. This was certainly an overloaded ferry. But the women around me were laughing and chatting, quite unconcerned. 'I might as well relax,' I thought, so I smiled at the ladies, scratched the goat's neck and tickled a fat diaperless baby's tummy.

Kobad's take on it was, "*Inshallah*, you sink or you don't."

The Bengalis used their push-shove, helter-skelter, avoid-falling-into-the-water technique to disembark. They grabbed their animals and kids, hurrying off to nearby villages or up jungle trails, in the same way city people rush off from subway trains.

I jumped off the raft at a tippy corner, but got so involved with disentangling my sari skirt that I lost sight of Kobad. In that one black moment, I panicked. What if something dreadful had happened to him? I was a foreign woman alone, my escort had all the rupees, I didn't know the way to the village or how to get back home.

I froze in place, on the edge of tears.

"Memsahib, the trail is here." It was Kobad calling and waving from the top of a small incline.

I hurried onto a path which had been recently chopped out of jungle thicket. The bush stubs tore at my sandals and stabbed my heels. Kobad, in the lead, hardly noticed.

"Good shortcut," he called.

"If this is good, what will the rest of the trip be like?" I muttered. The heat and humidity were beginning to press like an ether mask. I groaned as I stopped to pick a sticker out of my heel.

Kobad heard me, turned around, and said, "Not to worry. Ride come too soon."

We passed by a stream where mothers, their saris glued to their bodies, were bathing their babies, and themselves. A young boy scrubbed at a bony water buffalo that swept the water with its broom-like tail in protest. Other children splashed and screamed as they floated on overturned clay water pots. I could imagine these kids in any swimming pool in America. They were just kids having fun.

"Hurry, Memsahib. Bus just now coming."

It was a hippopotamus of blue metal, belching black smoke and bulging with passengers. We were ignored until Kobad yelled and waved wildly. Gradually the bus came to a slow, the driver expecting us to grab on as it crept ahead. I managed to swing onto the rickety steps, but got tangled in my wretched sari. The bus jerked, and I lurched forward, landing in a basket of chickens. Three chickens squeezed up around me, gargling and ruffling at my intrusion. By the looks of the jammed bus, though, I didn't have the worst seat. Kobad didn't even have a seat. He hung on to the hand rail, half in and half out of the bus, with his feet toeing the step.

Ten miles down the road the bus jerked to a stop. Passengers scrambled over the top of me to get out.

"Come, Memsahib," Kobad called.

I couldn't wiggle free without squashing the chickens. And with the chickens' owner glaring at me, that would not be a safe thing to do. The flustered poultry and I would have appreciated his help, but, of course, being a Muslim man he would not touch this foreign female in public.

Impatient to move on, the bus driver took charge. He grabbed the side of the basket and dumped us out. The chicken owner grabbed his fowl, stuffed them back in the basket, and huffed off. I skidded down the bus steps to land on my backside in the dust.

A quick brush-off and we were on our way again.

"Are we almost there, Kobad?" I asked, more whining than hopeful.

"Too soon, Memsahib," he answered. I groaned, fearing what his "too soon" meant this time.

"Only one more water."

He had not said ferry, nor boat, nor bridge, just "water." One more river to cross.

Were we supposed to swim across? My feet were burning, the sari in total disarray. At least I'd be cool. But I could hardly meet Kobad's villagers in a dripping sari that clung to my legs like blood suckers.

"Water come too soon." Kobad's call sounded eager as he pointed ahead to a shallow stream.

He lifted his lungi and waded in, sandals included. He didn't look back at me, knowing that I would need to hoist my sari, or soak it.

But without turning around, he called back, "They are waiting for you, Memsahib. See?"

I stopped at the water's edge to look up. The tidy little village huts of dried mud walls and leafy roofs were strung with shiny paper and swinging tinsel. A large sign at the entrance, in big red letters read *WEL-CUM MEMSAB*.

I was thrilled. I was honored. And then I was worried. What did they expect me, a Memsab to be? How could I be what they expected when I didn't know what it was? Kobad and I should have discussed this. Too late now. He was already hurrying up the hill.

I slipped off my sandals, tucked them under my arm, and toed cautiously into the soothing wetness. As I felt my way across the stream, contemplating what my demeanor should be, my bare toes stubbed against a rock.

Down I sprawled, flat out.

"Koba-a-ad," I wailed. But he was already out of sight.

So I just sat in the water, trying to collect myself. 'No question what they will think of the *Memsab* now. Why did I ever agree to come? How presumptuous of me,' I whimpered to myself.

A very few minutes later, a gaggle of sari-clad village ladies splashed into the water around me. They sat down, looking at me, at each other, giggling. An elder *ama* lifted the scarf end of her sari to dab gently at my face and arms.

Then I saw why they were giggling. Ama's scarf was turning black. My light green sari was taking on a dark stain. My arms were becoming splotched and striped. I was turning into a zebra! The temporary black hair coloring was running.

When I thought how shocked proper Begum Halani would be when I told her this story, I started to laugh. The ladies began to laugh, too. We had that water churning as everyone helped wash the black dye out of my hair and clothing. All of Begum Halani's efforts to make me what I was not, had failed.

But I was still going to have to get out of the water in that dripping garb, and go up to meet the other villagers—the men.

Ama pulled me back when I tried to stand. She motioned for one of the young girls to run up to the village to get a dry sari.

With amazing precision, Ama wrapped that five and one half yards of fabric around my waist and lower torso, even as she removed my wet blotchy green one. No prying eyes of the village men would be viewing this memsahib's body! The sari felt really secure. The blouse was wet and stained, of course, but with the dupatta pulled up across my chest and over my shoulder, my wet bosom was modestly hidden.

We walked up the trail together, my wet sandals sucking as I stepped. When we entered the village, Ama turned me over to Kobad, who was too polite to laugh. Not so, Jahir Bux. He shook his head and snorted, thoroughly enjoying my discomfiture.

"Where is your family, Jahir Bux? I'd like to meet them," I said, trying to ignore his fun-poking.

Three little plump, giggling girls trooped out to stand in a row like tin soldiers. The one boy, a teen-ager, slouched behind his sisters. He looked down, frowning.

I salaamed to each child as they said their names. "Jahir Bux, don't you have another daughter? I would like to meet her, too."

"She does not want you to see her, Memsahib, because she is very black. Black in my country is no good. Too hard to marry off such a one. But she will come if I tell her. Zarina, come to me."

The child, who had been peeking from behind a hut, scuffed up the dust with her bare feet as she sidled over to stand by her sisters.

She was a beautiful little girl, probably eight years old. Her skin was a shining ebony that matched the luminescence of her dark eyes. She had a pixy face and long curly hair that refused to stay in proper braids, like those of her sisters. My heart went out to her because she would have to struggle against discrimination all her life, despite her beauty. If she had her father's feisty spirit, she might be able to overcome it. This thought gave me new appreciation for my bold cook.

The women who had been at the river with me lined up for an official welcome. I never did get straight which women belonged to which men, or if some of those women were the wives of one man. I had long suspected that Jahir Bux had a "city wife," as well as more than one village wife, hopefully not in the same village. Muslim law does permit three wives if the husband can treat them equally well.

Ama came to stand next to Kobad. She was holding a baby girl, a little doll whom Kobad proudly introduced as his daughter. She had curly black hair and gray eyes like her daddy's. I reached out for her, but she screamed in terror of this stranger. Kobad excused his wife's absence, saying that she was ill today, confined to her hut. That usually meant that she was having her menstrual cycle, so I just nodded.

Kobad's father was propped on a stool which was tipped against a building. He fanned himself with a banana leaf, ignoring my greeting.

Then he began a tirade to Kobad about Memsahib's *pani*. Kobad explained that his father thought that I considered myself too good to drink village water. So Kobad had to explain that the weak white memsahib would get sick if she did not carry her own special water.

When it was time to say goodbye, Ama loaded me down with mangoes from their laden tree, more than I wanted to carry, but I couldn't refuse such graciousness.

My expectations of rural Bengalis in their own village had been hazy because my experiences with them had been in a medical capacity, not personal in the way this was. Whatever expectations they had of me could not have included a clumsy, dripping, striped, black-then-red haired foreigner who was wholly inadequate to their simple village lifestyle.

I got so much more than they did. These were beautiful, generous people who treated me with kindness. I would rather have visited their village than to have attended a maharajah's wedding at his grandest palace.

CHAPTER 27 **SHOCK CONTROL**

The World Health Organization truck and jeep rolled into the center of a neat bamboo-lined village a few miles out of Dacca. Doctors, interpreters and health workers like myself jumped out and began setting up tables, laying out supplies, preparing to immunize the entire community against typhoid fever. Just up-river some new typhoid cases had shown up, so villagers were eager for protection. They were soon shoving and pushing at each other without any attempt at organized line-up. With an interpreter's help, they were divided into three groups: mothers with children at table 1, men at table 2, women and old or debilitated people at table 3.

The village leader, Abdul, stood for his shot first, to show the others how easy it was. The medic who was giving the leader's injection used the military type of injector which gives shots speedily. When the injector device was pushed firmly against Abdul's arm it went "pop." Abdul slumped to the ground, believing he had been shot by a real gun. The villagers scattered like blowing leaves in a typhoon. It took another half hour to convince the apprehensive group to return to their line-ups. We went back to the familiar syringes and needles; no more popping injectors.

My line for injections was table 1, mamas with babies and small children. After each one was immunized he or she received a wrapped hard candy. One mischievous little fellow tried to swipe a fistful of candies on his way by. I needed to take a break so I grabbed the youngster's hand, walking him with me, away from the line—and the candy. He didn't speak English but I got that his name was Ali. I watched as he skipped off to the rice paddy, while I headed for the W.H.O make-shift latrine. The villagers used the paddy fields, but that wasn't for me. I needed a seat.

I was returning to the immunization line when I saw Ali again. He was holding his arm up, eyes scrunched, reluctantly accepting his fate.

"Hey, Ali!" I yelled, "You already got your shot. You only get one."

This time his mama was standing behind him, looking very stern. The doctor, about to stick in the needle, pulled back. Mama shoved Ali almost into the doctor's lap, scolding in rapid fire Bengali.

An interpreter soon discovered the problem. This child was not Ali, but Abu, Ali's identical twin. Twins were rarely found in Bengal. If born to very poor families, the weaker of the two babies might be sacrificed or sold, so that there would be enough food for the healthier baby. It would take a strong-willed mother like this one to save that second child. Perhaps it was because they were boys, and as such, had more value. Girl twins would have been considered too costly to keep.

A few weeks passed and I was bored with my routine Consulate Office work: handing out aspirin, stamping immunization cards, looking down throats of local employees who feigned sore throats in order to get the sweet lozenges available for that ailment.

One morning I received a call that an outbreak of cholera had occurred in a river village near Dacca. The Pakistan-SEATO* Cholera Research Lab, which had only twenty beds, one nurse and three research doctors, was being inundated with patients and their families.

I was apprehensive about going out to the Lab because I knew absolutely nothing about the disease, had never seen a case of cholera, and didn't know if I could be of any assistance.

But, I could at least go out to offer my help.

As I drove up to the Lab, I had to creep along to avoid hitting the many families who were milling about in front of the small building. The rain was bucketing down. People hunkered under make-shift blanket umbrellas, or shrank in against the rough brick walls.

Inside, stoic women rocked their retching children or soothed groaning relatives lying nearby. The place reeked of draining body fluids. I stepped over patients to get to the nurse for instructions.

"Hi, I'm the acting American Consulate nurse," I said. "Can I be of any help?"

She glanced up from the patient she was tending, gave a curt nod, pointed to a table of intravenous fluids and sets, and said, "Yes, you can start an IV in this man's arm. If you can't find a vein, and you probably can't, use the larger needle and infuse the fluid under his skin."

One look at that cadaverous patient, and I questioned my ability to keep from jabbing into bone. His skin looked like mummified leather. He rolled, releasing liquid bowel contents into a hole cut through the canvas cot for buttocks accommodation, at the same time, vomiting into a bucket on the floor.

I forced the needle through the drawn skin of his thigh, praying that he could absorb enough fluids to save his life. As I watched, his tissues began to pillow and spread like a dry sponge filling with water.

"Are you through there?" A doctor leaned across the cot to hand me a cup. "Find someone who is not vomiting," he said, "and help him sip this electrolyte fluid. Get him to swallow as much as he can."

On a cot behind me was a patient who was not rolling or vomiting. I put the cup to his mouth and he pulled at it thirstily.

"Take little sips so you won't vomit," I said, as I showed him what I meant.

He sipped and sipped until the cup was empty, then held it up for more. As he downed that second cup of liquid, a transformation began to take place.

The skeletal being I had thought to be a man, was a woman.

She lay back, exhausted, and I turned to help another patient. When I looked back again, she had pulled her garment close around, and was wobbling toward the door where her family was waiting for her.

I drained the fluids her body had left behind and cleaned off the cot for the next patient lucky enough to have care in this research treatment center.

Southeast Asian Treaty Organization

Author's note: Through the research studies at this Center, much advancement in understanding of cholera and its treatment, has taken place. Today, better methods are used to give villagers clean water and sanitary conditions, and new vaccines promise longer immunity. Rehydration treatment can be started more quickly in areas where intravenous solutions are scarce, and antibiotics are more readily available.

CHAPTER 28 **DARING DELECTABLES**

A short time after my couple of days at the Cholera Lab I was still feeling shocked and drained. I couldn't stop thinking about those agonized cholera victims. The epidemic was tapering off though, the Cholera Lab nurse had told me this morning. They wouldn't need my help now.

I leaned back against the fat pillows on my sofa, and listlessly paged through an old copy of some British magazine. A cooking column caught my attention.

BLACK ANTS FOR TEA TIME

"In Colombia, fat black ants are fried in butter to be eaten as crispy snacks with tea or cocktails."

Sounded good to me. Here in Bengal there are black ants aplenty. I shook off my lethargy and hurried to the kitchen. With Jahir Bux away on holiday, the kitchen would be mine.

I whipped out the fry pan, melted some water buffalo ghee, and ran to the garden for a scurry of juicy black ants. Fast as I threw them into the sizzle pan they began taking their leave. I pushed in. They crawled out. The few I managed to corral frizzled down to minuscule black etchings. The others were running all over the kitchen. 'Quick! Out with the insect spray before Jahir Bux returns.' The article continued with

"In the Camerouns, basketsful of termites are collected by small Camerounians who, after having plucked off the wings, wrap the termite bodies in banana leaves. The small bundles are then set over hot ashes for crisping."

'If small Camerounians can do it, I ought to be able to,' I thought. 'Don't much like the wing plucking part, though.'

I went ahead and wrapped squishy little bug bodies in banana leaves, like the article said. Aluminum foil would have been better because the bugs in the leaves never did get crisp, and the ones that fell out, which were most of them, had the bitter crunch of ashes.

'So far, not so good, but there's one more suggestion to try, while I'm being creative.'

> *"The Congolese revel in boa constrictor, which they cut into slices and grill over a grass fire."*

Bengal has pythons. They are constrictors, too, and probably quite tasty. Pythons are huge traffic stoppers. I watched one stretch all the way across a two-lane road to dip its head into a flowing canal. An impatient ricksha driver rolled right over the snake's back, but caused not even a ripple in its mottled skin.

I tried a very small python, thinly sliced and generously spiced—didn't even burn all the grass in our back yard. But my over-sensitive gardener quit, anyway.

Enough of that cooking column. I was finished with derring-do in Jahir Bux's kitchen. That column wasn't the one to inspire the cook to serve us more creative meals, but we all wished that something would. I tried to give subtle suggestions for additions or changes, but he ignored them.

The U.S. Information Service had been giving a month-long training series for household workers, especially food handlers. Jahir Bux had refused to attend on the grounds that he already knew "that stuff." But when he discovered that the last one of the series was to be <u>Ways To Become A Creative Cook</u> he trotted right on over to the meeting.

The family was delighted about his attendance, but we didn't see any changes from the usual boring meals...until Sahib's birthday. We were treated to a delightful dinner of sautéed butterflied prawns set on a bed of coconut milk-flavored rice with fresh pineapple rings, and crisp ten-inch-long green beans—a major departure from the slimy okra he tried to hide under bitter tomato sauce. We almost cried with the joy of it all.

Sahib, not given to great praise of the cook's usual fare, was so pleased that he called Jahir Bux to come out of the kitchen for a special 'thank you.'

"Coming now, Sahib," the cook answered.
But he didn't come.
Sahib called again.
"Just now coming , Sahib," he responded.
Again, we waited, but no Jahir Bux.
"NOW, JAHIR BUX, NOW!" yelled my impatient spouse.

After another brief period, the dining room door swung wide as our illustrious cook came through, balancing a beautiful chocolate cake on a cardboard platter. This, he swung down grandly in front of Sahib. Its lettering said:

HAPI BRTHDY
S O B

Jahir Bux spells everything phonetically...or not.

CHAPTER 29 **DR. CHAND'S SURPRISE**

The first thing I noticed about Dr. Chand was the intelligent sparkle in his dark eyes as he leaned forward over the conference table, intent on every word being said.

We were attending a medical conference in Dacca, where each attendee was to present a medical paper or discuss his particular role in helping to advance health measures throughout the area.

Obese, pompous Dr. Salaam, surgeon, read in sing-song, mind-numbing style, the latest procedures in removal of intestinal tumors. At the conclusion of his treatise, he remained in front of the audience, bushy black eyebrows raised in expectation of his much-deserved applause. His jowly face glistened. His too-tight western shirt sucked sweat like an inkblotter. He rocked, heel to toe, heel to toe, waiting until a few "Here-Here's" and finger-tip clapping allowed his pontifical nod, and a chance to sit.

A German missionary doctor told of his success using plastic surgery for leprosy victims, and to re-build the faces of Muslim women whose noses had been cut off as punishment for adultery. Several Muslim attendees made coarse noises and scraped their chairs hard on the terrazzo floor, making an angry show of disapproval as they marched out. Although the government frowned on the practice of face-maiming, there were those in some family groups who meted out punishment as in generations past. The German doctor folded his papers and left the room, to the applause of those of us conferees who remained.

When it was Dr. Chand's turn, he cleared his throat and straightened the stiff collar of his neat Nehru jacket. He did not go to the front of the audience as the other speakers had done, but stood modestly by his chair to introduce himself.

"I am Dr. Chand," he said in cultured British English. "My hospital is small, but it serves the needs of my somewhat scattered Hindu community. Of course, any patients are welcome. Until three years ago I was taking my studies in Britain, with the encouragement and financial help of my people. I vowed to return to those who needed me so that I could repay them with the latest in Western medical practices, as well as our traditional Eastern methods. Any counsel from you, my prestigious colleagues, will be greatly appreciated."

He bowed his head and slipped back into his seat.

Polite murmurs went through the group. Minimal applause.

My part of the program was to describe the involvement of the American Consulate with the local immunization program. Being a foreign woman and a mere nurse, I was surprised to receive a patter of applause. They were probably grateful that the talk was short.

Soon the conference broke up into small cluster groups. No one included Dr. Chand. But I was not included either, so I asked the Hindu doctor to tell me more about his hospital. He was a gracious man, pressing my hand in Western style and inviting me to visit his village to see for myself.

"My village is in the mofusils, but it is not so far, only maybe thirty miles. If you will come, I will be showing you my surprise." His face glowed with ruddy brightness when he said, "surprise."

"What kind of surprise is it?" I asked, my curiosity roused.

"Ah, you will be knowing when you visit. Yes, you must come."

The following week I had a few days free so I decided to go to the Hindu village to learn Dr. Chand's surprise.

The aggressive driver of the bicycle ricksha I had chosen to ride in, gave his little ding-a-ding bell a workout as we careened through the narrow streets of Old Dacca. All in our path were in jeopardy: bare-torsoed water carriers, lumbering water buffalo, beggars and urchins. I felt like a passenger in a Roman chariot race.

The ricksha finally stopped at the Brahmaputra river landing, where a raft, the so-called ferry boat, crashed against the shore as people and animals, bicycles and carts were shoved aboard. I, too, was pushed into a tiny space to pray for the miracle that would keep this thing afloat. Periodically we had a wave-washing, but miracles occur often in Bengal. No one fell off or got swept away. Nor did the "ferry" sink. We were poled safely to the other shore of this ancient river expanse.

The next leg of my journey was by bus. I was pressed next to two saucer-eyed youngsters, who howled if I glanced at them. I was a trained pediatrics nurse and got along so well with children in my own country, but Asian kids were scared-to-screaming of me. It hurt my feelings.

Young boys clutched the outsides of the windows or climbed on top of the vehicle for a free ride. The driver's door remained open, letting in petrol fumes and billowing puffs of road dust.

After an endless, withering ride, the bus driver brought the vehicle to a neck-jerking stop.

"Memsahib, out!"

The driver sounded like he was throwing me off the bus. But he was waving and pointing to the path that led to the Hindu village. I knew this was the end of the second leg, and the beginning of the final leg, which was, in fact, "by leg."

As I scuffed down the narrow bullock trail toward the Hindu village, my throat parched, my stomach ready for an ulcer, I wondered if Dr. Chand's surprise was worth this misery. Had I fallen for some imagined mystique?

Just ahead stood a tidy little village of mud and bamboo huts, fanned and shaded by graceful coconut palms and tall bamboos.

Children playing in the nearby paddy saw me first. They ran, shouting, into the village. Soon all the villagers hurried to greet me with their "*nomaskar*," greetings, hands together, heads bobbing. These I returned the best I could, clumsy by their standards.

"Dr. Chand's hospital?" I asked.

The lead man of the village pointed to a slight hillock where a low, white-washed building stood, like a temple blessing its surroundings.

"Hah gee, Doctah Chand," he said, with a vigorous nod.

"Ah, Doctah Chand, Doctah Chand," echoed the villagers.

I followed behind the head man up the well-trod trail to the hospital.

The villagers followed me, quietly and respectfully, unlike the usual entourage of noisy, curious on-lookers.

"Doctah Chand!" the lead man called.

"Doctah Chand, Doctah Chand," the villagers echoed.

Doctor Chand walked slowly down the verandah steps to meet me. He was dressed in a long loose white shirt and smoothly wrapped white lungi. He looked dignified and impeccable. I looked down at my sari skirt that had been splashed with river water and layered in red mud, felt the moisture under my arms and the grime on my face.

The gracious doctor ignored my appearance. "Come, come. It is so kind of you to visit my village, my hospital. Now you must see."

We walked through a large ward that he showed me could be divided into individual rooms for male or female patients. The walls and floors were spotless. Everything smelled fresh. Patients in the two private rooms were lying on clean cots. No dirty linens or cooking utensils lay about, as were commonly seen in other hospitals. The sparkling latrine, the doctor explained, was available to patients only, another departure from what I had seen elsewhere. This hospital was one of the very cleanest I had seen in East Pakistan. It was a delightful surprise, worth the difficult trip.

"You would like to be washing up a bit before we take tea," Dr. Chand stated. He clapped his hands and a young woman wearing a fresh white sari appeared with a *loti*, a pitcher of cool water. We walked out to the verandah, where she shooed the curious villagers away. Then she poured water over my hands to rinse off the dust. It would take a lot more than that to clean me but I did feel refreshed and ready for tea.

"Ah, now you shall sit and relax to have your tea before I take you to see the surprise." Dr. Chand's face gleamed in anticipation.

"More surprise?" I asked. "I thought the cleanliness and serenity of this tiny hospital was *THE* surprise."

"Thank you, but oh, no! You must see."

Eager now, I chugged my drink, gobbled the sugar biscuit and stood, ready to see.

We walked together down a short trail to a lower level room.

"We have poisonous snakes here, you know. Our most deadly snake is the *krait* (pronounced krite). It is small, not easy to see, gives no warning, and if disturbed will strike at anything in its range. Its venom paralyzes the victim in minutes. I have been unable to save such a victim because the nerve center which controls breathing has been poisoned.

"A colleague in Britain has sent me a possible solution."

He swung open the door of a heavily-walled room.

"Here it is!"

Standing alone in the center of the room was an Iron Lung.

"*An Iron Lung in a tiny remote village of Bengal!*" I forgot to breathe.

When I could talk again, I said, "Dr. Singh, this is remarkable! How many patients have you been able to save? Why didn't you mention this at the conference?"

He shook his head sadly. "They would only have laughed. They know that I cannot use this wonderful, life-saving machine. We do not have electricity."

He turned to me and smiled. "Some day we will be having a generator. Then I will have something to tell them."

CHAPTER 30 **ONE VERY HOT NIGHT**

After two and one-half years working with—sometimes it felt like working for—Jahir Bux, the family had accommodated reasonably well to his ways. We recognized that his inflated ego made him believe that he was the best cook in all of Dacca. I had learned the limits of his tolerance for Memsahib's menu suggestions, and in general, he had been much more cooperative since his rabies scare.

There were times, though, when I tested the limits. One day, I said, "Jahir Bux, Sahib asked me again this morning why we didn't have any curry meals. He would be so pleased if you would make him a nice chicken curry for dinner."

Cook rolled his big brown eyes until mostly just the white part showed. He emptied his lungs in a deep sigh and shook his head.

"Memsahib, I am telling you many times. Why you do not remember? This *pukka* cook does not make *kari*! Village woman make *kari*."

That evening a group of our ex-pat friends were lolling around in boredom, when someone mentioned that he wished he had some curry something.

My husband jumped in with, "Me, too. We'll get Jahir Bux to fix us some. He thinks he's the world's best cook. Let him show us. Go ask him, will you, Joyce?"

"Not me. I just put in a curry request for today's dinner, even using your name as bait, and still got thoroughly put in my place. Why don't we try the curry and *tikka* down at the Chinese Tea Gardens? My lady friends tell me that their curried and barbecued foods are better than the Pakistani cooks make. And they do serve "special tea!"

"Yeah!" yelled the collective gang, as they raced out the door.

At the Gardens, we pushed tables together at one corner of the patio to accommodate our boisterous group without disturbing other diners.

"We would like three large bowls of vegetable curry, with rice of course, and chicken *tikka* for all of us."

The waiter nodded, turned to leave, but turned back, and with a big wink, he said, "Plenty much special tea of the house?" This said very fast for the benefit of other patrons.

We were soon diving into gaspingly hot curry, and gnawing on spicy barbecued chicken, while we gargled down our tea by the potful.

We had just gotten a good grasp of this meal when a couple of policemen walked through the archway of the patio. They surveyed each table from their positions by the gate. We continued our conversations and eating, pretending to ignore their surveillance.

I started to cough. "They had better leave soon, or I'm going to choke to death," I whispered to my neighbor. "My teapot is empty and I don't dare ask for more while those guys are here."

One of the cops fingered a wave as the two men went back out the gate, apparently having done their duty.

"Waiter!" yelled my neighbor, "we need more special tea."

We finally finished our meal, tipped our host generously, having left in our wake, a cemetery table full of gnawed chicken bones, empty curry bowls and many, many dainty, drained tea pots that smelled suspiciously of beer.

We, now very hot-mouthed, very happy bunch of expatriates, returned en masse to our house for an evening of dancing and frivolity.

When Jahir Bux came in to work the next morning, he saw the mess from the night before.

"Memsahib, you did not tell me you were going to have a party." He gave me a dark look, accusation in his glare. "What you eat?" He stopped glancing around the living room, and tromped out to the kitchen.

"It's OK, Jahir Bux," I called. "We didn't dirty up your kitchen. We just had a little party here after we had eaten at the Chinese Tea Garden. Their vegetable curry and chicken tikka were VERY good!"

"Huh! Memsahib, why you not ask me? My chicken tikka is best in all Dacca. Tea Gardens tikka, bah!" If he had had feathers, they would have been ruffling.

"I didn't know you made chicken tikka. Will you write down your recipe for me so that I can share it with friends when I return to the States?" Rumpled feathers smoothed.

Jahir Bux's phonetically written,

SHIKEN TIKLA
1 shiken, kilt and kilin
Katt 4 piss owt of skin
Soke 4 owers in mext of:
4 tese mex cary spaic
1 capp sower milik (water buffalo milk)
4 tese salat oyl
Kokit char kol

Translation: CHICKEN TIKKA (Barbecued Chicken). This recipe is for the pigeon-sized Pakistani chickens.

Kill and clean one chicken.

Cut into 4 pieces and remove the skin

Soak (marinate) for 4 hours in a mixture of curry spices:

1 1/2 tsp. curry powder   1/2 tsp ginger
1 tsp. cayenne pepper   1 tsp salt
1/2 tsp. garlic powder   1/2 tsp. turmeric
1 cup sour milk   2 tsps. salad oil

Cook slowly over charcoal, turning often, and basting with marinade until chicken is golden brown and tender.

Serve with chappatis (Pakistani flat bread) or whole grain tortillas, and copious amounts of cold beer. If you are still standing, you may complete the meal with a tossed green salad and pineapple sherbet, but don't be fooled into thinking anything but the beer will cool down the heat.

CHAPTER 31 **THE RED CARPET**

Sue and Joe, the new Comilla Project advisor couple, had moved to the Foundation guest house after a brief stay with us. Their "ten childs," (Habib's tease) was just one adorable red-haired four year old.

Sue and I still went everywhere together as she adjusted to the tropical climate and the Bengali culture. She admired the architecture of some of the ancient buildings, ignoring their moldering decay. She often laughed about how her husband had swept her off her feet, promising that "someday they would live in a palace as fine as a maharajah's." I noticed that, just as I had done, she bought heavy "old brass" items such as small boxes and filigreed lanterns to decorate the new home she so patiently waited for.

One morning Habib called to ask if I would join Sue at his office. "...about the Comilla house." He hesitated. "She maybe will need your help."

As always when Habib asked, I tried to oblige. Sue was already at the office, sipping the hot sweet tea that was the ritual greeting of hospitality.

"Memsahib Taylor," Habib addressed Sue. "Good news. Your maharajah's palace is almost ready for occupancy. You may choose furniture from our warehouse, and order fabrics for curtaining and pillow covers, plus a new carpet for the salon, in whatever colors you wish."

Sue's mouth gaped. She frowned. She blinked. And finally, she stammered into, "Is that really—or just a figure of speech?" She was asking me, not Habib.

"You do mean 'maharajah's palace'—right, Habib?" I scowled at him. Once upon a time, I, too, had visions of maharajahs' palaces with all their romantic trappings. Two-plus years later, I knew better. I didn't want this sweet, unsuspecting young woman to be wakened too soon from her fantasy.

"Of course, Memsahib, you know I do not tell you untruths." But here came the old neck waggle that meant anything its waggler wanted it to mean.

Sue's fair skin glowed pink as she shyly asked Habib, "Can Joyce go with me to visit my—my palace? She can help me decide which furniture and colors to choose."

"Of course, why not? Abu driver, will take you. He comes from that district. Jahir Bux will fix your lunch to carry along. Take plenty water."

The four-hour trip, about sixty miles from Dacca, included an open ferry large enough to accommodate the car. Breezes from the wide expanse of the Meghna River were so refreshing that I almost forgot the niggling apprehension I had felt about the reality of this palace. Habib would not have called me without a reason.

Sue bubbled on with her plans to order shimmering gold draperies, pillow covers in turquoise and gold silk, and as much brass and teak as possible. "And at last I will have the big red carpet I've always longed for!"

"Abu," she leaned across the back of the front seat to ask the driver, "have you ever seen the palace? Is it very big and beautiful?"

"Hah-gee, Memsahib. Many times I see palace. Very big. Very old." Abu's usually animated voice was monotone. His head waggled as though it were on a metal spring.

Comilla was an ancient town in a large district which, until the British got involved, was the property of only one land owner. This palace had been his home. But for many years after his death the building was vacant. Then it became a warehouse. Only recently, Ford Foundation had leased it to renovate for the new agricultural advisor and his family.

As we drove through town, Abu waved at friends along the narrow street. We came into a residential area where the very old houses, snug behind proper picket fences, were in serious decline.

Soon we stopped in front of an orchard-sized, unmanaged yard. Standing toward the back of the garden was a wide, dilapidated white-washed brick building. It appeared to be propped up by many bamboo ladders. Painters were balancing on them, trying to reach high spots with long rag-ended poles. Gobs of white-wash splashed to the ground as they swabbed over great patches of black mold. Several pieces of brick siding had broken off, the bricks lying in heaps nearby.

Sue stared around. "Abu," she said in a weak, quivery voice, "why are we stopping here?"

"Maharajah's Palace, Memsahib. Too much very old."

She swallowed hard, pursed her lips, and said, "Well...then let's go see."

I went, too, of course. But I was feeling her let-down, practically in tears for her. I wanted to brain Habib for dragging me into this mess. Seems like he could have found more desirable housing. He wanted me to encourage her, but by the look of the place it wouldn't be easy.

Anyway, I tried. "These guys aren't nearly through. They will soon have this place looking quite grand. Just getting this garden expanse cleaned up will make a huge difference, don't you think?"

Sue looked over at me with a half-smile. "Oh, ya," she muttered.

We had to walk carefully as we neared the palace. The bricks of the walkway and the steps leading up to the arch-roofed verandah were broken and scattered.

At the entrance to the main salon, we stopped to admire the beautifully carved, but sagging, front door. Inside the room, painters were putting on the finishing touches of vivid bilious green paint. An overpowering acrid smell of mildew plus paint chemicals knocked us back.

I gave Sue my handkerchief. She wiped her eyes and gave her nose a mighty blow. "Well, at least they are working on it."

She looked around the room, at the walls, the windows, the floor. "Maybe it's this filthy old carpet that's smelling up the place," she said.

I called Abu, who helped us roll up the grimy rug and drag it outside.

"Look! It's a marble floor." Sue danced around, as she kicked away piles of dust left behind by that ancient carpet. "I believe this place can become beautiful. We'll get rid of that ghastly green paint, dress up those shabby windows, and—and—I think—yes, definitely! a large red carpet will look smashing in this salon. I do so want that carpet."

'Good for her,' I thought. 'Anyone else, including myself, would have burst into tears. But not this lady. She promises to be a trend-setter.'

Many of the rooms were in wretched condition: ceilings drooping, paint peeling, windows broken, all requiring a lot of time to repair. But three of the bedrooms, two bathrooms and the kitchen were already almost in good enough shape for this little family to occupy.

Back in Dacca, we stopped at Habib's office for Sue to order fabrics, paint, and a very large red carpet. She bubbled excitedly about her plans for the palace.

Habib looked at me and mouthed, "THANK YOU."

I smiled my sugariest. "Your workmen have a lot to do yet, *Mister* Habib. I know you won't let up on them until everything possible is done. Will you, Sir?" I wasn't mad at him anymore, but he did deserve a bit of tweaking.

Joe happened into the office while I was still there, and Sue immediately told him about her great plans, laying out through her imagination, how beautiful their Maharajah's palace was going to be. I noticed that she down-played how dreadful it looked right now.

Joe patted her lovingly. "Little wifey mine has a real artistic touch with decor. What she does will look elegant, I can assure you."

Habib sat at his desk, watching the couple, and listening. He smiled over at me, just a little smile, and nodded, Western-style.

We were about to leave when a short-term American consultant stormed through the office door and over to Habib's desk.

He started pounding on it, and yelling, "Habib, where is that damned permit you promised me two weeks ago? You people never get anything done around here. I've gotta get out of this stinkin' country. Permit—Permit—Give!" He stuck out his hand so far that it almost hit Habib's face.

Habib flushed, eased open a narrow desk drawer, took out a square of paper to which he signed his name with a slow deliberate swing. He stamped it firmly with a gold seal.

"Here," he said, as he held it out to the scowling man. "This will get you into Nepal. Have a pleasant trip, Sahib." Habib looked down at the desk as he spoke.

"Hmph, it's about time," the other man answered, as he grabbed the document. He turned to Joe. "You're new here, aren't ya? See? Ya gotta be tough to get anything done around here."

He stomped out of the office.

We Americans looked at each other as the Ugly One left, all of us wanting to apologize to Habib for the man's obnoxious behavior.

"How do you keep so cool, Habib?" I asked. "How do you do it?"

Habib grinned his sideways grin, "I'm used to it by now," he said. "We Asians have our ways. We have our ways." That neck waggle again.

Several weeks passed before the Taylor family and all their newly chosen furnishings and supplies headed for Comilla. The red carpet would be coming from Karachi, West Pakistan by train, a thousand miles across India. "In about two weeks, Memsahib," Habib had told Sue.

One month later, Sue phoned me from Comilla. "Joyce, am I being too impatient? I haven't heard anything at all about the carpet. Shouldn't it be here by now?"

I told her I would check into it for her.

When I asked Habib, he waggled his head, looked wise and pronounced, "Just now coming on the train to Dacca. Then onto a truck for Comilla—big carpet, you know. Coming soon."

Seven days passed. Habib called me. "Please to do a good thing? The carpet for Comilla was stolen by dacoits when it was being off-loaded from the train. I do not have the heart to tell the young memsahib. But please to say I have re-ordered."

Aw, me again? I hated to be the messenger, but Habib often helped me, and he was my friend, so I let him wimp out. Sue just sighed her acceptance of the delay.

Another two weeks, another call about the carpet. But this time Habib called Sue himself to tell her the good news. "I have been informed that a red carpet is on its way to Comilla for you. Watch for it."

Sue's voice crackled with excitement when she called to tell me. "Please come visit right away. You can see what we have done to this place so far, and you can help me re-position the furniture around the new carpet."

My driver had just stopped us in front of Sue and Joe's palace, when a bicycle ricksha rolled up next to us with a "Ding-ding-ding-ding."

Sue came running down the steps to greet me, but the ricksha driver stepped in front. "You Memsahib live here? This carpet belong you." He jerked his head in the ricksha's direction.

"Where's the truck?" she asked. "Where's the carpet?"

"Only me here."

He took a small red door mat from the seat of his ricksha. "This you carpet," he said, as he flagged it in her face. "Bakshish, now." When she didn't respond, he dropped the mat on the step, and marched back to his bike.

Sue, howling her frustration, heaved the mat at the delivery fellow, who scrambled away, frantically ding-dinging his little bell as he rode off. She ran back into the house to rage through the phone at Habib's secretary that she needed to speak to Joe, "NOW!"

Abu and I waited outside until the storm had subsided.

As I heard the story later, Joe had rushed into the office in a panic that something dreadful had happened to his wife or his child.

After the heated telephone recitation from Sue, he pounded on Habib's desk, shouting, "What kind of game are you playing with this carpet business, Habib? My wife is furious, and I'm sick of it!"

Joe admitted to me that he knew he had behaved just like that other ugly American, "But, really! It has just been too much."

Habib, he said, had promised to order again.

Six months went by. No red carpet came. The Taylors purchased small Persian rugs they could take back home when their tour was up. Sue's draperies of "shimmering gold silk" became delicate Dacca Muslin, a fine quality cotton, substituted because the gold silk, according to Habib, was no longer available. The additional decor of brass and teak was lovely and fitting for Sue's Maharajah's palace, although not quite as elegant as Sue's imagination promised, had a large red carpet been included. No longer was there even a hint of "re-ordering" a red carpet.

Shortly before our three-year tour in East Pakistan was finished, Sahib and I were invited to a housewarming celebration at Habib's new home. We had gone out several times to follow its development, but only when it was still in the basic brick and mud-wallow stage.

When we drove up to the place for the party, we weren't sure we'd come to the right address. The house looked absolutely palatial. It had a freshly white-washed and decorative brick front, a generous wrap-around verandah and wide inviting steps. Polished carved-wood double doors opened into the marble-floored foyer. Sounds of sitar and tabla drums floated toward us as we walked toward our hosts.

Habib, whom I had never seen wearing other than casual Western-style attire or an occasional business suit, had an air of royalty about him...his garments of fine white embroidered cotton, perhaps, but mostly it was his assured, dignified stance.

His plump, demure wife wore a red sari of embroidered silk, heavy jeweled earrings, and one shining gem at her throat. She stayed modestly behind Habib as he greeted us with a warm, confident "*nomaskar!*"

A bearer, in a white lungi uniform, bowed slightly when he took my shawl. As I watched him glide away on slippered feet, a fingertip tickle of frost trailed across my neck.

This was my fantasy from three long years ago. But this was real. My Maharajah, his palatial surroundings, the seductive music, the silent slippered servant, all here. They had been here all the time, and I had been too busy, too self-involved, to find them. How many other things had I missed for lack of caring enough? Three years of daily surprises, sorrows, and insights, and all I knew is that I had missed far more than I had learned.

Habib broke into my reverie. "Memsahib, please to come into the salon for refreshments."

As we stepped into the party room, my husband and I stopped short, shocked.

The room shimmered in flowing gold silk draperies, glittering sequined turquoise floor pillows, carved teak tables, filigreed brass lanterns, and on the floor...*a very large red carpet.*

I could only shake my head and stutter, "Ha-Habib."

He shrugged his shoulders and grinned his sly, sideways grin.

"We Asians...you know."

His deep brown eyes met mine, head on, and he knew that I knew.

****

EPILOGUE — FAREWELL TO BENGAL

Our luggage stood next to the boot of the grey English Ford that would take us to the Dacca airport. The men in their white uniforms were lined up nearby, just as they had been when they were first introduced to us as our "servants." We knew them now as our employees, our helpers, our friends.

Kobad was holding something behind his back. He shyly handed me a foot high orange and black clay elephant. "To remember you the Hindu mela, Memsahib," he said, as he rubbed the wetness from his cheeks.

"You won the elephant, Kobad! And you are giving it to me? Thank you so much. It will always give me good memories."

Jahir Bux stepped out from the line to hand me a small parcel of recipes.

"No kari recipes, Memsahib. This pukka cook not..." This "*pukka*" cook picked up the hem of his freshly ironed apron and blew his nose. Good thing his nemesis, dhobi Hassam, wasn't present.

Joseph, the mali of the garbage incident, had fashioned a finely-woven necklace to which he had added fragrant frangipani blossoms. I slipped it over my head for all to admire.

Ashok Ali, as emotional as the others, gave his "commandant" Sahib, the sharpest salute of his life. To me, it gave visions of Kipling's Gunga Din.

They all smiled fondly at Steve, their Chota Sahib. Kobad had taught him how to make a "fighting kite," using crushed glass on the string. Jahir Bux had saved him, and the household, from the "bad luck mongoose" by bringing in a "good luck parrot." Joseph had cleaned up the yard after Steve's boat building had finished. Ashok Ali kept to himself, the night escapades of the young sahib.

These were all good men, and faithful employees to whom we could give honest letters of recommendation and generous enough bonuses to help them until their next employment. They would probably be "offered" by Habib's office to work for the next advisor family to move in.

Only now did I realize what it must be like for them. Every two or three years, they each had to adjust again to new and quirky ways of another new and quirky sahib and his memsahib. The tears they shed, although probably not crocodile, were as much for loss of their security as for the love of their employers.

It was doubtful that we would meet again, but not impossible, because Sahib had accepted an extended position with Ford Foundation, in Pakistan's West wing. Our new living quarters would be in Lahore, one thousand miles across India, when we returned after a month of vacation.

I took a long last look as we drove away. How normal it looked to me now as compared to how it had seemed when I first saw the high compound walls with their barbed wire tops; then the heavy metal gate, the salute by a uniformed guard, our attention drawn to a troop of white-uniformed men, whom the driver called "servants."

The solid, white-washed brick house we first moved into was the same as today, still with the bars at the windows. At that time, we wondered if we were captives, or were we being protected, and if so, from whom?

Never once did I feel like a captive, or worry about the danger of harm to our household. If we needed that protection, I didn't know about it. We were always warned when it was wisest for us to stay at home because of some religious or political zealots' activities.

Any threat to my life was due to my own lack of cultural understanding or my over-adventurous spirit.

The Bengalis, in general, those who showed anything beyond brief curiosity, were reserved but always polite. Those we met in more social circumstances were chatty and charming. They loved bright colors and lively dancing, were artistic in drama, poetry and art. They tended to express their emotions in highs of great joy, and lows of deepest melancholy. Like Jahir Bux, they "suffered."

The Punjabis of the Lahore area were said to be more stoic, less given to creative impulses. Everything was opposite between the two wings of the Pakistan nation: the climates, languages, attire, food, even seriousness of Islam. It was said that the only thing that tied the two sides together was Pakistan International Airlines.

Habib was at the airport to see that all our papers and tickets were in order, a job he handled with complete efficiency, as he had done for us three years before.

As we were saying our goodbyes, I saw him slip a small package into the side pocket of my purse. He glanced at me, gave a brief sideways grin, and was gone.

When I had a quiet moment to myself, I opened the little gift packet. Inside was a delicate silver filigree necklace. The note with it read:

"You are carrying away the heart of Bengal—and my own. Please remember us well," Habib.

Never Cheat A Holy Man

ABOUT THE AUTHOR

Joyce Mueller, now in her 90's, remembers how it felt to be a Caucasian, English-speaking, non-Muslim, nurse, wife, and mother confronting a totally opposite culture. She went from scared and shocked to empathetic and appreciative. Now widowed, Mrs. Mueller lives on the southern Oregon coast. She is still writing poetry and stories about her further travels and adventures in West Pakistan, in the Solomon Islands, in her native North Dakota as well as the exotic Pacific Northwest of the United States.

Made in the USA
San Bernardino, CA
14 July 2016